Boys from the Blackstuff

STUDIO SCRIPTS

Series editor: David Self

Working
City Life
Communities
Situation Comedy
Love and Marriage
Power
School
Situation Comedy 2
Scully *Alan Bleasdale*
Boys from the Blackstuff *Alan Bleasdale*

For details of contents, see pages 280-281

Boys from the Blackstuff

by Alan Bleasdale
Edited by David Self

028860

STUDIO SCRIPTS

Hutchinson
London   Melbourne   Sydney   Auckland   Johannesburg

Hutchinson Education
An imprint of Century Hutchinson Ltd
62–65 Chandos Place, Covent Garden, London WC2N 4NW

Century Hutchinson Australia Pty Ltd
PO Box 496, 16–22 Church Street, Hawthorn, Victoria 3122, Australia

Century Hutchinson New Zealand Ltd
PO Box 40–086, Glenfield, Auckland 10, New Zealand

Century Hutchinson South Africa (Pty) Ltd
PO Box 337, Bergvlei 2012, South Africa

Acknowledgements are due to J.M. Dent & Sons Ltd for
the use of a quotation from *Do Not Go Gentle Into That
Good Night* by Dylan Thomas; and to the British
Film Institute, Bob Millington and Lindsey Boyd for
permission to quote from BFI Dossier 20: *Boys from the
Blackstuff,* edited by Richard Paterson (BFI Publishing
1984)

Set in Century Schoolbook

Printed and bound in Great Britain by
Anchor Brendon Ltd, Tiptree, Essex

British Library Cataloguing in Publication Data
Bleasdale, Alan
    Boys from the Blackstuff.—(Studio scripts)
    1. Readers——1950—
    I. Title   II. Self, David   III. Series
    428.6   PE1119
ISBN 0 09 159681 5

Contents

Introduction

A silence descends on Anfield. The Liverpool footballer, Sammy Lee, prepares to take a corner. In the moment's hush, a young boy's voice is heard. 'I can do that.' The crowd roars in delighted recognition at one of its latest hero's catch phrases.

The fact that the hero, Yosser Hughes, and his regular utterances, 'I can do that' and 'Gizza job', should have so quickly passed into public awareness in the autumn of 1982 was remarkable; even more so as Yosser was not the star of a peak-time comedy show but the manic anti-hero of a series of bleakly honest plays about unemployment and its attendant crimes and tragedies, set in Liverpool about the time of the Toxteth riots, and shown on BBC2 late on a Sunday evening.

It was of course partly due to the superb acting of Bernard Hill who played Yosser; it was also due to the clarity of vision and brilliantly realistic writing of the author, Alan Bleasdale.

Alan Bleasdale
It was while he was a teacher that Bleasdale began to write. Finding a lack of any relevant 'readers' for his teenage pupils, he began writing the Scully stories, Scully being a street-wise Liverpool lad about to leave school. These stories were subsequently broadcast on local radio on Merseyside and on

Radio 4, and Scully also featured as the hero of a BBC 'Play for Today', *Scully's New Year's Eve*. Later still, Alan Bleasdale dramatized the stories for television and they were first shown on Channel 4 in 1984. (The scripts are published as a companion *Studio Scripts* volume.)

Since giving up teaching to concentrate on writing, Bleasdale has written radio plays (such as *Love is a Many Splendoured Thing*, commissioned by BBC Schools Radio and published by Hutchinson in *Act One*, edited by David Self and Ray Speakman), and also many stage plays including the West End success, *Having a Ball* (set in a vasectomy clinic). He has also been a co-director of the Liverpool Playhouse.

It is however as a television playwright that he is best known.

The Black Stuff

It was in this play (produced in 1978 and transmitted in 1980) that Bleasdale first wrote about the group of characters who feature in *Boys from the Blackstuff*. In *The Black Stuff*, Chrissie, George, Loggo and Yosser, together with their foreman Dixie and his eldest son Kevin, are a gang of tarmac-layers. They are working away from Liverpool in Middlesbrough, employed by McKenna. While they are there, Chrissie, Loggo and Yosser are approached by a group of gypsies to work for a local farmer during the hours they are being paid by McKenna. Yosser talks the others into the scheme even though they must invest their savings in it. Subsequently, while Dixie is involved in a row with a clerk of works, Yosser, Chrissie, Loggo and also George slip away to work for the farmer. McKenna arrives by helicopter, guesses what is happening and threatens to sack Dixie. McKenna finds the others (by seeing them from his helicopter). He is determined to sack Yosser but George becomes angry and provokes him into sacking them all. That night, Dixie and Kevin leave the others, refusing to speak to them. The following day, when the rest of the gang is due to be paid by the farmer, they find the gypsies have cheated them out of their pay and also their investment. When Yosser tries to pursue the gypsies, the van runs out of petrol.

Boys from the Blackstuff

Following the making of *The Black Stuff*, Alan Bleasdale proposed a series of plays about the same group of characters but on the theme of unemployment which was becoming an increasingly serious problem on Merseyside (as it was elsewhere). The original plan was for a seven-part series, with episodes about each of the main characters in *The Black Stuff*:

1 Chrissie's story;
2 Dixie's story;
3 McKenna's story;
4 The Social Security employees;
5 Yosser's story;
6 Loggo's story;
7 George's story.

Six 'outlines' were commissioned and approved. Bleasdale went ahead and wrote the first three scripts by February 1980. For various reasons, it was impossible to go ahead with production for two years. After a year, perhaps because the BBC wanted to show it was still interested in the series, it was decided to detach the self-contained third script (McKenna's story) from the series. It was filmed as *The Muscle Market* and was first shown in January 1981.

Later that year, by which time new production facilities were available (see page 10), unemployment and the particular problems of Liverpool were even more urgent and the two 'single' plays had had considerable success, it was decided to go ahead with *Boys from the Blackstuff* as a series of five fifty-minute plays. Bleasdale wrote the remaining scripts, but what was now the third script (originally called 'Pulling the Plug Out') was rejected. (It involved Chrissie and Loggo leading the DoE officials on a comic chase round Liverpool.) Subsequently, it was replaced by 'Shop Thy Neighbour'. One scene, set in a pub, was kept from the original and included in 'George's Last Ride'.

Production

Over recent decades, television drama has been made either in a studio and recorded on video tape or filmed on location. Obviously some film, location-made inserts have been included in studio-based dramas, but basically there have been these two distinct production methods. Video production is much cheaper but has been disliked by many involved in its production because studio sets are rarely as realistic as location settings and because (it is generally agreed) it is artistically less satisfying. Although four or five video cameras may be involved in a single scene, only one series of images is recorded on tape. The decision of which shot or angle to keep must be made at the time of recording. When a play is filmed, there is time to edit different shots and takes at leisure after shooting, in a process that can be highly creative and artistic in its own right.

Boys from the Blackstuff developed new techniques in television drama production (and the wait for the necessary equipment was one of the reasons for the delay in its production).

David Rose, then head of the BBC's English Regions Drama Department at Pebble Mill, and Michael Waring, the producer of the series, were keen that it should be made on location but money was not available to make all five plays on film. However, in 1981, Pebble Mill took delivery of a new lightweight outside broadcast video unit, and this was used to record four of the plays on location. Two portable electronic cameras were used, each feeding its pictures to a separate video tape recorder. As with film production, the final selection of shots and editing of the plays could be done in comparative leisure after recording. 'Yosser's Story' was made on film for a variety of technical reasons.

Though the scripts are undoubtedly the creation of Alan Bleasdale, the plays were the product of a collaboration between author, producer and the director, Philip Saville, one of the pioneers of British television drama. The collaboration can perhaps be best understood by considering how they each assessed the others' contributions:

Anyone who worked with Philip would know that his contribution was massive, but he's a very different man to the likes of Bernard Hill (Yosser), Mike and me. He was absolutely the right man for the job because he brought a distance to it. He brought somebody more used to flying to Corfu and California than walking down Smithdown Road. He gave it a distance and he's a brilliant maker of pictures. We had major arguments! I had more battles with Philip than with anyone, but they were good battles. There wasn't petulance and jumping up and down; it was creative argument!

Alan Bleasdale

Alan is an exceptionally potent writer who knew his milieu and I'd no qualms to ask his opinion on things at the slightest provocation. I consulted him on casting, place, settings, meanings. I asked him to all the shooting, all the rehearsals, all the casting sessions. I particularly respected his sheer knowledge. I have a strong intuitive knowledge about the stuff of life and relationships. However, I didn't know too much about the Liverpool setting. It was essential that I found out as much as I could. He was very co-operative.

Philip Saville

That's one of the marvellous things about Alan. Mercifully when we've got a real problem like that, where one can't push the system any more, or you're up against a complete brick wall as we were with the site, it's very good to be able to go back. Alan can really think on his feet in those circumstances.

Michael Waring

Michael is the sort of producer you're glad to have around — very solid; a great contributor personally and a lovely producer with whom to kick ideas to and fro. However, he's a man steeped in logic. I'm a strong believer in the irrational. His logical reasoning at a time of crisis I sometimes found pedantic, but always something good came out of it. It produced a friction that was very creative. He's the most super guy to work for. It couldn't have happened without him. He was a fighter from the beginning. If a producer's fighting you, the director, no good will come out of it. A producer has got to fight for the director's needs.

Philip Saville

Reaction

As we have seen, the series was an immediate popular and critical success. It received a repeat showing (on BBC1) only two months after its first transmission. In 1983, the scripts won Alan Bleasdale the Royal Television Society Annual Award and the writer's award from BAFTA. The series itself also won a BAFTA award as the year's best series or serial and the Broadcasting Press Guild Award for best drama series. Bernard Hill won an award for his portrayal of Yosser and the series also won craft awards for its technicians.

Some understanding of why such a 'black' story should be so generally popular can be gained from a television interview with Billy Butler, then a disc jockey on Radio City, Merseyside's independent local radio station. He had featured the series at some length in his programmes.

Can you tell me what impact the series 'Boys from the Blackstuff' *had on you and your listeners?*

Personally, the impact it had on me was all-encompassing: from humour to fear. It frightened me a great deal and it showed me things I already knew and made me think a little bit deeper about them. Some of the violence I must admit frightened me a bit, like when the little girl butted the social worker. I would have said, 'Alan, you shouldn't have put that in', but there you are. And otherwise, with the radio thing — I mean, it's affected the listeners considerably. Yosser Hughes only existed for six weeks and is now part of Liverpool folklore. I mean, to be part of Liverpool folklore, you exist at football matches . . . and within two weeks of that series being on, Yosser Hughes was a Kop character. You know, every time someone scored a goal, it was, 'We can do that, gizza job, we can do that . . .'. The Liverpool goalie now has a reaction with the crowd every time he makes a save. The Kop chants, 'We can do that Bruce, we can do that'. And even the radio . . . we had a marvellous line because the Scouse people are quick thinkers and our humour is unique. Part of a quiz show I do, where we're not allowed to give any clues, so they have to just answer the question, the question we had was: 'What were the famous words that Lord Nelson said to Hardy as he lay dying on the deck of HMS Victory?' And the answer: 'Gizza job, Hardy, I can do that.' You know, it folds you up, it's as simple as that. He's just part of Liverpool folklore now.

Do you think the series was optimistic, or pessimistic?

Well, I think it was truthful. Pessimistic might not be the right word. Because it was truthful, it's hard to be pessimistic or optimistic, when what he is saying is right. And he brought home to people that being on the dole isn't just a phrase; it does affect your life. It makes you hide from people. It makes you ashamed to associate with people who are your friends. Even down to the littlest thing like not going to the pub because if they say to you, do you want a drink, you're scared to accept because you know you can't buy them one back, and you can't get any simpler than that. It's the shame of actually doing it. I think Alan might have gone in roundabout ways to emphasise it, but he brought it home.

What do you think made the series such a success?

I think it was a success where I live because it's where I come from. I think it was a success throughout the country because of its truthfulness — because it said things I don't think anybody else but a Liverpool writer could have said. I don't think they could have summed up the despair and also the humour that's connected with today's situation as well as we can. I mean, people think that in

Liverpool sometimes we get big-headed, but we're not — we're proud. And I think on simple things like understanding human nature and human feelings and just humour itself, we understand it better than anybody else.

That interview was recorded by John Archer for a BBC television programme made to coincide with the repeat transmission. In the same programme, Alan Bleasdale was asked why he wrote the plays:

I think the thing to remember about this series is that I didn't write it for the bishops and knights and queens and kings and people who have got castles. I wrote it for and about the pawns and I don't actually really care what people think about it, as long as those who are down there who have had to suffer unemployment, accept and acknowledge and like it. That was the basis behind it.

Would you like to think the series could help . . .?

Well, I always thought that a typewriter was a pretty small weapon to throw at the problems of the time. I don't quite think that now. I think possibly that sometimes the typewriter or the pen can be mightier than the sword if you get it right. But I still don't expect any change, because I don't think writers have that purpose in life, and I think all I can do is show and get people to understand. If then they understand, then there might be change, but people who know me well know I'm a pessimistic sod and I don't hold out a great hope for change. But if the reaction I've had is any indication, I think that we will get understood.

When you think back over the series, what scenes do you feel most pleased with . . . on the screen?

Well, I think the things that moved me most, I mean I think everybody will remember Yosser's Story, and they have a right to, because Bernard Hill is an actor of tremendous quality — certainly among the top two, three actors of his generation. But I think, having said that, the most important character in the play is Chrissie, because Chrissie is the common man, the kind of bloke we all know. I mean, everyone knows a Yosser, and we all move out the bar when Yosser arrives. But Chrissie is the fella you have a pint with, who is quiet and gentle and generous and peaceful. And what I have tried to do with Chrissie, with the common man, is to see through his eyes what was going on and for him to fight back. So Chrissie, for me, is the most important character, because Chrissie represents all of us and what he does in the series is to take his coat off and say 'All right, boys, where is it? I'm going to fight back,' and that was the only message of hope in it for me.

The fact that *Boys from the Blackstuff* (and especially Yosser) have become something of a cult, even a commercialised cult, should not be allowed to distract from its importance. At one level, it is simply a very powerful picture of a particular society but, as the Anglican Bishop of Liverpool, the Rt Reverend David Sheppard has said, 'It's (also) about people with great gifts and abilities being robbed of a chance to use them.' Perhaps even more importantly, it has helped a number of unemployed people to realize that unemployment is not their fault and has helped them to recover some pride and dignity.

The Storylines

Jobs for the Boys

Back from Middlesbrough and some years on, 'the boys' attempt to survive unemployment in job-starved Liverpool. While signing on, Chrissie receives a tip-off that an Irish building contractor, Malloy, is looking for an 'unofficial' gang of workers to work on one of his sites. Chrissie assembles a gang which includes Loggo and Snowy Malone, one of George's sons. Snowy is as politically committed as his father and is angry that they should have to work 'illegally'. Chrissie tries to persuade Malloy to make their employment official and Yosser arrives, asking to be taken on as a brickie. Meanwhile, two Department of Employment investigators are attempting to catch anyone who is claiming unemployment pay while actually working. When they eventually raid the site, comedy turns to tragedy.

Moonlighter

Dixie Dean, still bitter about the Middlesbrough episode and still unemployed, is drawing the dole but working at nights as a port security guard. On board a ship, he is persuaded to turn a blind eye to a robbery. At home he receives a summons to the Department of Employment and realizes that someone has informed on his wife who has a part-time job delivering leaflets. He rows with his children, including Kevin who has now given up looking for a job. A DoE investigator calls, posing as a saleswoman; and, under pressure from all sides, the once upright Dixie becomes further involved in theft at the docks and receives a share of the proceeds but loses much dignity.

Shop Thy Neighbour

Following the Malloy incident ('Jobs for the Boys'), Chrissie's dole has been stopped until there has been an enquiry. Short of money, he rows with his wife, Angie, (partly because she is angry with him for giving food to the pets he keeps in their back yard while his children are hungry). Against this, we see the problems faced at home by Miss Sutcliffe, the head of the fraud section of the DoE: she has to cope with a mother suffering from senility. We also discover some of the conflicts, indignities and pressures suffered by those who work in the fraud section.

With the gas supply now disconnected, Angie and Chrissie row again and Chrissie locks himself in the bedroom. George (meant to be in hospital) arrives in a state of collapse and wants to stay to help them but an ambulance arrives to take him back to hospital. DoE investigators (except Moss, who has resigned in protest at the futility of his job) arrive in pursuit of Malloy whom they arrest. After a drinking spree, Chrissie tries to talk to Angie but another row leads to his breakdown.

Yosser's Story

After waking from a nightmare of drowning himself and his three children, Yosser visits the DoE where he is told he is entitled to draw more benefit. He fails to understand and we see him at home and wandering around Liverpool with his children. An attempt to persuade his wife, Maureen, to return home takes place outside the flat of her latest lover. Predictably, it fails.

His home is visited by a series of officials, intent on

collecting debts or concerned about the welfare of his children. Eventually, Maureen reclaims her furniture, the children are taken into care forcibly and against his wishes, and he is evicted. He deliberately gets himself arrested but escapes custody to plunge into the lake seen in the opening nightmare.

Though we meet other characters from earlier episodes (including George who is now seriously ill), this play concentrates on the story of its central character: the collapse of a man of immense energy and thwarted ambition who is unable to articulate his problems and emotions, a man driven to self-destruction.

George's Last Ride

Not far from death and unhappy in hospital, George Malone regularly discharges himself to visit places as diverse as the dole office and the grave of his son, Snowy. Knowing that he will refuse another major operation, the doctor and his wife agree that he should return home to die, so far as is possible, in peace. His other sons, John and Ritchie, return home for his last days as well, while he resumes his informal neighbourhood advice service.

Chrissie takes him, in his wheelchair, on a tour of the landmarks of his working life and George dies quietly where he used to work, in the once busy Albert Docks. His funeral is attended by very many people and after the traditional family 'wake', Chrissie and Loggo go to the pub. There they find a very different atmosphere. As the landlord tells them, the unemployed have nothing to do but get drunk, and Chrissie and Loggo despair as a party of workers who have just lost their jobs set about drinking their redundancy pay.

Using the Scripts

The most informal group reading of a playscript is helped by rehearsal. Even a very experienced professional actor prefers to look over his or her part before a first reading in front of their colleagues. In a classroom or drama studio, therefore, those who will be reading should be given time to look over their lines: to make sure that they know when to pause, when to 'interrupt' the previous speech, and to work out the changing mood of their character before they are asked to read aloud.

It is much easier to read effectively and convincingly to a group from a standing position or from one where you can be seen by your audience. It may be helpful to appoint a 'director' who will decide the location of various settings and rehearse the actors in basic movements, checking that they know when and where to enter and exit.

Note that it is possible for a group to break into smaller groups, and for each of these to rehearse its own interpretation of one or more scenes, and then present their versions in turn to the whole group.

For this edition, some of the film directions have been modified so that these directions (along with scene titles and descriptions of settings) can be read aloud by a narrator. It might be helpful if he or she were in view of the 'audience' but away from the acting area. Note that, provided these directions are read sympathetically, a television play will read as fluently in the classroom as will any other kind of play; but it should not be forgotten that (like any good television play) it was conceived in visual terms. It will therefore be fruitful to discuss (as Philip Saville, the director, did with Alan Bleasdale) where and how each scene should be 'shot' to realize the writer's intentions.

A number of other discussion points and projects are suggested on pages 274-279.

Viewing the plays

The Black Stuff and *Boys from the Blackstuff* are available *for hire only* to educational and similar groups, from the BFI Film and Video Library, 81 Dean Street, London W1V 6AA.

The Black Stuff is available on 16mm film and on VHS or U-matic cassette.

Each episode of *Boys from the Blackstuff* is available, on video cassette only (VHS or U-matic).

Please telephone 01-734 6451 for present fees and for bookings.

The novel based on the series, *Alan Bleasdale: Boys from the Blackstuff*, by Keith Miles is published by Granada Publishing.

Michael Angelis as Chrissie in Jobs for the Boys

Jobs for the Boys

First shown on BBC2 on 10 October 1982

Characters

Chrissie Todd
Loggo Logmond
Yosser Hughes
George Malone, Chrissie's uncle
'Dixie' Dean (really, Tommy Dean)
Kevin Dean, Dixie's son

At the Department of Employment
　Donald Moss }
　Lawton 　　} two fraud section officials
　Chrissie's clerk (female)
　Loggo's clerk (male)
　Dixie's clerk (female)
　Yosser's clerk (male)
　George's clerk (female)

At the building site
　Snowy Malone, George's youngest son, a plasterer
　Malloy, a building contractor
　Jimmy Johnson
　Policeman
　Arthur
　Council worker

Yosser's children
  Jason
  Anne Marie
  Dustin

Jobs for the Boys

---

1 Department of Employment building

We establish the Department building. A series of shots: two workmen; a girl in white talking to a man; a man with bucket; the girl in white and the man; a Rastafarian. We see the DoE building. We hear the traffic going past.

2 Department of Employment building

We see the interior of the DoE. Two general points of view show clerks at work. We see **Chrissie**, *and we are aware of the* **counter clerk** *who is behind a wire mesh grille. We see* **Chrissie** *and the others in turn through this grille. Like caged animals. Each is interviewed by a different clerk.*

Clerk: Name.

Chrissie: [*Misses a beat*] Christopher Todd.

Clerk: Full name. [*Takes out a file*]

Chrissie: [*Quietly*] Christopher Robin Todd. [*Shrugs*] It was me Mam. [*Turns head*]

[*Freeze*]

[*We see* **Loggo**. *He is looking at his gold watch, and is expensively and well dressed*]

Loggo: Wha'? Course I want a job. I'm desperate. But look, no offence meant like, but we've been through all this before an' well, y' have already made me miss me golf lessons.

Clerk: Look, these matters take time ...

Loggo: What I'm sayin' is, get a move on, will y', cos I'm supposed t'be at the Haydock races for half-past two. There's a good boy.

[*Freeze*]

[*We see* **Yosser** *with his three* **children***. He is leaning forward*]

Clerk: The procedure of a test check is just a formality, Mr Hughes. However, I'm afraid —

Yosser: Afraid? Y'll be terrified in a minute. [*Leans in*] Now sort me soddin' Giro cheque out before I knock y' into the disability department.

[*Freeze*]

[*We see* **George***, who appears to be dressed in working clothes, but we can only see the top half of him*]

Clerk: If you could just wait there, Mr Malone ...

[*She goes to the filing cabinet*]

George: Come on, girl. I should've been on site half an hour ago.

Clerk: [*Hesitant*] Yeah. [*Opens filing cabinet*]

George: [*Backing away*] I don't like to let the boys down, you know. I mean, there'll be ten ton of the black stuff on the deck by now, waitin' for me.

[*We see the* **clerk***, then* **George***. He is wearing pyjama bottoms and slippers*]

[*Freeze*]

[*A row of men are waiting on a bench. Another row of men are waiting at the counter. We see* **Dixie**.]

Clerk: Dependants, Mr Dean?

Dixie: Yeah, a wife and four kids. Two at school and two on the dole.

Clerk: Ah yes, but unfortunately the two on the dole don't count for —

Dixie: No one on the dole counts, friend.

[*Freeze*]

[*Two men peer through a barely open door leading to the interior offices of the Department. The door has a sign — 'UNEMPLOYMENT OFFICE' — which is the euphemism for the fraud section. Both men are in their thirties and are wearing stock fashionless office suits. The younger of the two who will emerge as the driver* **Lawton** *mutters to the other one, his passenger* **Moss**. *They come out*]

Lawton: [*Driver*] Hey, there's one of them. Todd.

[*We see* **Lawton's** *point of view of* **Chrissie**. *He focuses on* **Chrissie**. **Moss** *joins him at the door, then walks off. We come back to* **Chrissie**]

Clerk: It seems from your files, Mr Todd, that one of our inspectors has visited your house on two separate occasions during the past ten days without receiving any answer.

[*We see* **Moss** *watching* **Chrissie**]

Chrissie: Ah, what a shame.

Clerk: You were out?

Chrissie: Looks that way, doesn't it?

Clerk: Can you tell me where you were?

Chrissie: I might be able to if you tell me when you called.

Clerk: It's the . . . morning of Tuesday the third, and . . . the afternoon of Thursday the twelfth.

[*There is a pause*]

Chrissie: Haven't a clue.

Clerk: Were you employed during those two days?

Chrissie: Who, me?

Clerk: Look, have you got a job, Mr Todd?

Chrissie: Oh yeah, I just come here f' the company and the pleasant surroundings.

Clerk: [*Patiently, and not without sympathy*] You haven't answered the question.

Chrissie: [*Looking away*] I haven't worked in over a year.

Clerk: Right, Mr Todd, that's all.

[**Chrissie** *stands*]

Clerk: We will, however, be making further visits to your house in due course.

Chrissie: I'll bake a cake.

[**Chrissie** *walks away. We hear the* **clerk** *call the next contestant*]

Clerk: Next.

[*We see the DoE hall at work.* **Chrissie** *walks towards the entrance*]

3   Entrance hall of DoE building

A man, **Arthur,** *is waiting.* **Chrissie** *comes from the hall into the doorway of the building, and sees* **Arthur** *with his back turned, facing a window ledge. He is looking down at the racing section of the* Daily Mirror, *marking off some horses with a pen.* **Chrissie** *approaches him, and stands beside him. He looks over his shoulder at the paper.*

Chrissie: Carnations are red in Albania this winter, comrade. [*He winks at* **Arthur**]

Arthur: Say that again Chrissie.

Chrissie: Ah, y' all right. You got anythin' for me? [*He puts his arm around* **Arthur's** *shoulder, and stares down at the paper*]

Arthur: Malloy's been askin' after you. [*Looks at* **Chrissie**]

Chrissie: That's nice of him. Go on.

Arthur: Bricks and wheels.

[**Chrissie** *nods*]

Arthur: Fourteen notes.

Chrissie: You're on.

[**Chrissie** *nods again.* **Arthur** *looks behind him for a second, then gets an envelope out of his pocket as* **Chrissie** *looks behind himself as well*]

Arthur: The van'll be at the end of your road in the mornin'. The keys'll be in the teapot on the dashboard.

[**Arthur** *gives* **Chrissie** *the envelope.* **Chrissie** *puts it in his inside pocket. They focus on the racing section.* **Chrissie** *points at the paper. He moves round*]

Chrissie: Teacher's Pet in the 3.15.

Arthur: Ah, well, I don't follow the horses, Chrissie. I only look at this so that . . . [*He looks behind again*]

Chrissie: I'd bet my life on it. In fact I'd go so far as to say it was an absolute certainty.

[**Arthur** *looks at him, then at the paper, then back at* **Chrissie**]

Arthur: How do you know that?

Chrissie: It's yesterday's paper. [*He half turns back*] Y'd never make a spy, Arthur.

[**Chrissie** *pushes* **Arthur** *and goes out.* **Arthur** *leaves too*]

4 Wasteland; before dawn

Chrissie *gets into a Transit van. He takes the keys and a note out of the teapot, and starts the van. He reads the instructions and drives off.*

5 Traffic lights; early morning; just before dawn

We see **Chrissie** *in a 30-cwt Ford Transit van. He is on his own. Then we see a Morris Marina van behind the Transit. It swerves to follow the Transit. But this is not a big moment, it is not dwelt on.*

6 A housing estate; early morning; a few minutes later

The sky is now a shade lighter. **Chrissie** *is driving slowly through a housing estate in the Transit van. He has the instructions in his hands as he drives.*

7 Wasteland

Chrissie *is driving across a patch of wasteland. Then he runs the van up on some waste ground towards the back gardens of a row of houses. As he gets out of the Transit, the Marina van parks nearby. Again this is not a big moment. Shadowy. If it is noticed at all, we shouldn't be certain if it is the same van as in Scene 5. We follow* **Chrissie** *as he starts across the wasteland. He goes past the remnants of an adventure playground with broken goalposts. There are three-legged chairs and mouldy mattresses lying on the ground.*

8 Jimmy Johnson's back garden

Chrissie *gets to the back gardens, and counts them quickly from one end of the row. When he finds the right garden, he tests the fence, but it won't give way or come loose. It is shoulder-height and there is a hole in it.* **Chrissie** *looks at the house which is all in darkness. He starts to struggle underneath the fence feet first. We hear a door being opened and shut quietly. We see* **Jimmy Johnson** *scurrying down the garden. He climbs onto the fence further down the garden.* **Chrissie** *is halfway under and stuck.*

Chrissie: Friggin' hell. [*He looks up*]

Jimmy: Very good. Our dog can't get through there.

Chrissie: [*Laughing*] Jimmy Johnson?

Jimmy: [*He nods*] Correct.

[**Jimmy** *vaults over the fence*]

Jimmy: Come 'head. We've only got three seconds before the searchlights hit us.

[*He moves away*]

Chrissie: Hey, give us a hand will 'y.

[**Jimmy** *comes back, pulls* **Chrissie** *out of the hole. They run across to the Transit*]

9   Loggo's house

It is still early morning, but is later and lighter again. We see **Loggo** *with a wicker-ware basket and three fishing rods. He is wearing waterproofs and a fisherman's hat with a couple of flights in the head-band. He saunters to the corner of the road, quietly singing 'Old Man River' in a bass voice with Alabama intonations. He gets to the alleyway that runs parallel with the main road he has been walking towards. He turns into it, quickens his pace, and heads towards the end of the alleyway.* **Loggo** *opens the back doors, enters the Transit and sits down.*

Chrissie: What's this with the fishing gear?

Loggo: Picked it up in the Shetlands. Nowt else t'do up there.

Chrissie: Ever caught anythin'?

Loggo: Yeah. Course I did. First go.

Chrissie: What did y' catch?

Loggo: Pneumonia.

[*Laughter. The Transit van moves off and turns right towards the main road. As it turns right we see the Marina start up and follow. The Transit turns into the main road and the Marina goes in the same direction*]

10   George's road

We see a small 'estate' of old-fashioned terraced houses, surrounded by a bleak new estate, backing onto the River Mersey at Dingle. The area is riddled with blocked-off roads and sudden cul-de-sacs. The Transit van comes into **George's** *road and goes down it for some distance. As it passes one of the houses we hear the horn beep once. The Transit continues for a while, then begins a three-point turn.* **Chrissie** *then takes the van back up the road. As he does so, the Marina van passes, going the other way.* **Chrissie** *stops his van, at the top of the road. As all this goes on, we hear* **Chrissie** *and* **Loggo** *inside the Transit.*

Loggo: This is George Malone's road, isn't it?

Chrissie: Yeah.

Loggo: How is he?

Chrissie: He's in hospital. I went to see him last night.

Loggo: How is he? I heard he's er y' know, sort of ...

Chrissie: Yeah, he is.

Loggo: Christ.

Chrissie: We're pickin' up one of his lads though, their Snowy.

Loggo: Ah no, not him! Not Karl Marx lives.

Chrissie: He's all right, Loggo.

Loggo: Oh aye, yeah. He's a barrel of laughs isn't he? I mean I just love listenin' to the latest production figures for sugar cane in Cuba. Especially when I'm havin' me dinner. I mean I'm sometimes that fascinated I let me food go cold.

[**Snowy Malone** *comes out of the house. He is a plasterer and he appears to have been recently battered. He makes no attempt at hiding his trade, and has his working clothes on, flecked and stained with plaster. His haversack is over his shoulder and he is carrying a large coil of rope. He is physically small, but walks like John Conteh used to at the end of a good round.* **Snowy** *walks towards the top of the* *road and the Transit. He goes past the Marina van which is parked just by a lorry on the other side of the road, having not yet started its three-point turn. The Marina van appears to be empty. As* **Snowy** *approaches the back of the Transit, he looks up at the bedroom windows in one of the houses and sees a curtain move. He turns quickly and catches a glimpse of a woman at her window. He stops, looks up and shouts up*]

Snowy: Yes, that's right. It's me again, love. Go ahead. Be a solid citizen. Do the decent thing and report me. Don't keep it a secret, whatever y' do.

[*The Transit comes backwards into vision as it reverses down the road. We see* **Loggo** *sitting inside*]

Chrissie: There's not much chance of that, Snowy. I mean, after all, y've just told the whole soddin' street y'self.

Loggo: Why don't y' buy a banner, bollocks? Or put an announcement in the Echo. Get in.

[**Snowy** *crosses towards the Transit as he talks*]

Snowy: It's her — the minge bag. The dole'll give her a retirement party by the time she's sixty, they will.

[*She drops her curtain.* **Snowy** *reaches the back of the Transit and seems about to turn and shout at the woman's curtains again.* **Loggo** *practically lifts him up into the Transit.* **Chrissie** *drives off*]

11   George's road/interior of the Marina

We see the Marina van, still apparently without driver or passenger. We hold on the Marina. Two men slowly come up into vision from the floor of the van (with no intention of it being comic). They are **Moss** *and* **Lawton**, *previously seen at the* *dole office. They are now in working clothes, donkey jackets and jeans. They clamber into the front seats.*

Moss: [*Flatly*] Well, that was good. I enjoyed that.

[*As the driver tries to start the van, the passenger pulls a cassette recorder out of his jacket pocket and speaks into it*]

Moss: Suspects have picked up . . . what's his name?

Lawton: Malone.

[**Lawton** *is still hammering the ignition*]

Moss: [*Continuing to record*] Malone in Freshfields Street and have turned left into Grafton Street. [*He switches the cassette player off and looks at the driver*] Y' goin' to flood that engine the way y' going on.

Lawton: I'm sure there's somethin' wrong with this, you know.

[*He gets the engine to turn over, but has the gears engaged in first. The van jumps forward, but just stops before it crashes into the back of the lorry, mainly because the passenger throws the handbrake on as he jerks forward and hits the windscreen*]

Moss: [*Politely*] Have you been driving long, Leslie?

Lawton: No, it's . . . [*He starts the car and discovers the reverse*] I'm not used to this one, that's all.

Moss: What was the number of the house Malone came out of?

[**Lawton** *crashes gears and pulls forward*]

Lawton: Dunno. But it'll be on record. I've followed him before. The little sod walked me all around town and then lost me in Mothercare. [*He rolls into the kerb*] No, y'see, I've er got an automatic at home, and it's . . . and it's hard to . . . [*He crashes the gears again*] . . . get used to the er . . .

Moss: Look, just get a move on, will y'? They'll be half way down the road by now.

[*We see inside the van as it slowly reverses*]

Lawton: We're all right — we know where they're going to end up anyway. Malloy's site. If we lose them we just go there.

[*He crashes the gears yet again and starts off towards the end of the road*]

Moss: Yeah, but it would be nice to see who else they pick up, and where. [*The car mounts the pavement*] You can use second gear, you know, if you want to. [*Second gear goes in painfully*] Not that it'll make much difference. All we're doing is catching tadpoles and tiddlers.

[*The van continues up the road, two wheels on the kerb*]

Lawton: Oh, I wouldn't say that . . .

Moss: [*Looking out of the window*] Do you know you've only got two wheels on the kerb? Ever thought about being a stunt driver, Leslie?

[*The car goes up and down the kerbs*]

Lawton: No. You see . . .

Moss: Don't. Y'll only make me cry. Just turn the corner and put your foot down. [*He misses a beat*] Y' right foot.

[*The van turns left at the end of the road. The right indicator is flashing. Tyres screech*]

12 Transit

The Transit van crosses over a bridge. Inside the van, **Jimmy**

and **Chrissie** *are in the front,* **Loggo** *and* **Snowy** *in the back.*
Loggo *is looking at* **Snowy's** *lumps and cuts. He grins at him.*

Loggo: Well then, who was it worked you over this time, Snowy? The boys in blue, the NF, the SPG, the CBI, the SS Fraud Section, the anti-abortion league . . .

Snowy: Y' don't know what y' talkin' about.

Loggo: Well tell us, anyway. I know y' dyin' to.

Snowy: No I'm not. And it wouldn't interest you.

Loggo: Yes it would, I like fairy stories

Snowy: They're not fairy stories, Loggo.

Loggo: Ah but still, go on, I still want t'know what happened.

Snowy: [*Primly*] As a matter of fact, I fell off me moped.

[**Loggo** *dissolves with laughter and* **Jimmy** *and* **Chrissie** *join in*]

13 Dixie's house

We see the back of **Dixie's** *house. It is a modern terrace with a small front garden, on the corner of a road. The Transit stops and parks on the corner of the alleyway.* **Chrissie** *gets out and goes to the back door.* **Chrissie** *knocks,* **Kevin** *opens the door. He is wearing a sweat-shirt and trousers and is even more battered than* **Snowy**.

Chrissie: All right Kev? Is y' dad — what's the matter with your face?

Kevin: Nothin' — compared with me ribs. And me dad's in bed.

[**Chrissie** *stares at* **Kevin** *for a second or two*]

Chrissie: But he's supposed to be doin' a couple of days with Malloy.

Kevin: Someone came for him last night. Twelve-hour nights somewhere. He's just got back.

Chrissie: Oh right. [*He half turns*] You'd better get back to bed as well.

Kevin: I haven't been yet. They've just let me out the police station.

Chrissie: Oh aye. Fightin' were y'?

Kevin: I wasn't — but they were.

Chrissie: The Brookvale gang?

Kevin: Nah, the Brookvale police.

Chrissie: Ah go 'way, Kevin — y' mean the police beat y' up for nothin'?

Kevin: Nah, it's a pack of lies, Chrissie. I tried to have it off with an elephant.

Chrissie: But what for?

[*Someone beeps the horn in the van.* **Chrissie** *looks away as he talks, then looks back*]

Kevin: Nothin'. I just happened to be there, that's all.

Chrissie: [*Doubtfully*] Yeah, well listen. Tell y' dad I called — I haven't really seen Dixie since, since that cock-up in Middlesbrough — y'know.

[*Now we see* **Dixie** *in a vest, opening the door wider*]

Dixie: Oh yeah. Y' mean when me and Kevin got the sack because of you cowboys. And couldn't get another job? Oh yes, happy days they were, Chrissie. [*He grabs* **Kevin** *away*] Thanks for the memory. Now frig off.

[*He goes to close the door*]

Chrissie: Ah come on Dix, we're all in the same boat.

Dixie: Yeah and you sunk it.

[**Dixie** *slams the door in* **Chrissie's** *face.* **Chrissie** *walks off*]

14 Road

We see the Transit driving along the road.

15 Transit

We see the Transit van back on the road. It is just starting off towards the main road.

Loggo: So why doesn't Dixie want the work?

Chrissie: He's got something else on, but he wouldn't work with us anyway after Middlesbrough. I don't think Dixie'll ever forget Middlesbrough. Mind you, neither will I.

Jimmy: Why, what happened in Middlesbrough?

Chrissie: [*Glances at* **Loggo**] Oh nothin' much. We just lost our life's savin's doin' a foreigner for two con artists.

Loggo: Yeah, an' Dixie lost his job, because it was his job to see we were on site with him.

Chrissie: Y'know, I would seriously like to bomb Middlesbrough off the face of the earth.

Loggo: Anyway, I don't know why Dixie's got a cob on with us for. I mean if he'd have been doin' his proper job we'd all still be workin'. In fact when y' come to think of it, it was all Dixie's fault.

[**Chrissie** *and* **Loggo** *exchange sour smiles*]

Snowy: What about his lad, isn't he havin' any?

Chrissie: He's not in any state to. He's been beaten black an' blue. By the police, he reckons. An' for nothin'.

Snowy: Well, that's about par for the course.

Chrissie: Ah, come on Snowy. I've heard all those stories, but I don't believe any of it.

16   Transit

We see the Transit back on the main road. **Snowy** *is in full passionate flow.*

Snowy: Oh eh, where've y' been all y' life? What were y' doin' durin' the Toxteth riots?

[**Chrissie** *doesn't answer*]

Loggo: Well, I was down the supermarket a lot.

Snowy: The police started that, y' know. 'Come here, Sambo, and suck this truncheon.' That's the main reason Toxteth went up, Chrissie. An' for every feller who dies in a police station an' gets his name in the papers, there's hundreds more who get a quiet little hammerin' down a dark alley an' crawl home to bed. I've been worked over too many times meself not to know that.

Loggo: Yeah, and I know what they did to y' an' all — they knocked y' brains out.

Snowy: It's fine by me. You make a joke out of it. But be warned, the way things 're goin' with this Government ...

[*No one appears to be listening.* **Loggo** *has his paper up,* **Jimmy** *is looking out of the side window, and* **Chrissie** *is staring at the road*]

Snowy: ... the swing to the right, tax relief for the rich, redundancies for the poor, mass unemployment, poverty, the curtailing of freedom startin' with the unions. It's all headin' for one thing — and one thing only — a fascist dictatorship and a police state!

Jimmy: That's two things.

Loggo: And it sounds just like Russia, Snowy.

Snowy: Oh don't be —

Loggo: Y'know you — you're an offence under the Noise Abatement Act.

Snowy: [*Looks out of the window*] All right, all right. But you give it eighteen months and ... [*He sees something. And sees what he wants to see*] Look, see, there y'are. The bloody law, and who've they got, eh? Two workin' lads.

[*We see from their point of view the Marina van. The men are just getting out, and two policemen are getting out of their Rover 3500*]

Snowy: Probably nothin' concrete to stop them for, just a bit of harassment, but that's how it starts.

17 Dual carriageway traffic lights

We see the Marina van and the police car. **Lawton** *is facing the two* **policemen** *One of the policemen is very very big.*

Policeman: Forty-eight miles an hour in a built-up area.

Snowy: [*Shouting out of the window of the Transit*] Bastards!

[**Moss** *and* **Lawton** *look at each other. The* **policeman** *glances at the Transit and goes to look away. But then he double-takes and grins as he sees the Transit come to a halt in the rush-hour traffic jam. He turns back to* **Moss** *and* **Lawton**]

Policeman: Wait there. [*He goes*]

Lawton: Where did they come from?

[*The* **policeman** *walks across the dual carriageway and then along to where the Transit is marooned. He gets to the back doors and opens them. He looks inside, stone-faced*]

Policeman: Who said that?

[*No one will look at him. They all point to* **Snowy**. *Then* **Snowy** *mumbles*]

Snowy: It was me.

Policeman: Get out here. Now.

[**Snowy** *gets out. The* **policeman** *towers over him by at least a foot and a quarter*]

Policeman: Tell me what you said again. Go on. What did you say?

Snowy: 'Bastard'.

[*The* **policeman** *goes down almost on his haunches to face* **Snowy**]

Policeman: Midget.

[*The* **policeman** *rubs* **Snowy's** *head affably, then turns and goes back across the road. As he goes,* **Chrissie** *and the others let their laughter out.* **Snowy** *goes to get back in the van. He mutters as he goes*]

Snowy: So . . . so. I can't help it. It's not my fault I was a premature baby . . .

[*We see the* **policeman** *arriving back. His colleague shows him an opened wallet with an authorized picture of* **Lawton** *inside.* **Lawton** *begins to protest*]

Policeman: Well, well, well, Geoffrey. We are honoured. Two sniffers from the dole. [*He looks them up and down*]

Lawton: I wouldn't quite put it like that, but it . . .

Policeman: Takes a good picture, doesn't he?

Lawton: Look. We are right in the middle of a very important investigation.

[*As* **Lawton** *talks, the second policeman passes his licence over*]

Policeman: [*He walks to the car*] Ooh, who's a naughty boy then? [*He looks at the front of the Marina*] Hey? Exceeding the speed limits, driving in a manner likely to cause an accident . . .

[**Lawton** *begins to protest*]

Lawton: Come on . . .

Policeman: [*Crushing* **Lawton's** *protest*] . . . and then just for luck, no 'L' plates on display.

[*The* **policeman** *tut-tuts.* **Moss** *shakes his head in total disbelief. The* **policeman** *starts writing the ticket as he talks*]

Policeman: I hope for your sake, Mr . . . Lawton, your passenger has a licence. A full licence.

Lawton: Look, er . . .

Policeman: Not like your one.

[**Moss** *takes out his wallet. Removes his driving licence and displays it for the* **policeman.** **Lawton** *dribbles on*]

Lawton: [*He walks to the police car*] You know, we work very closely with some of your boys, and we . . .

Policeman: [*Withering him*] Insurance?

[*The second policeman walks to the police car and gets in*]

Lawton: I expect it's . . . er it's . . .

Policeman: Produce your insurance document at your nearest police station within the next five days. If you would be so kind. [*He gives* **Lawton** *the ticket*] I was on the dole for eighteen months, friend. That's why I'm here today giving you a ticket. 'Cos I've met your kind before. [*He turns away*] Have a nice day. [*He gets in*]

[*The police car drives away. We see* **Lawton** *looking at them and then sneaking a look at* **Moss**]

Lawton: I didn't like his tone, y'know. I've got a good mind . . .

Moss: Get in. [**Moss** *pushes him towards the passenger side of the van*]

Lawton: I just thought, y'know, I'd put a bit of practice in. Me test's comin' up in a fortnight and I thought with having this job . . . [*He climbs into the van as he talks*]

Moss: Oh yeah all right, and you thought with me being new here, a woolly-back from Wigan, you could . . .

Lawton: Oh Donald, believe me . . .

Moss: [*As he starts the van up and moves away*] Just shut up, will you . . . We'd better go back and get this van changed. I don't know who they were calling bastards, but they're sure to have clocked us in this.

Lawton: I'm sorry, Donald, I am, really. [*He coughs*] You won't tell anyone, will you?

[*The Marina van drives off*]

18 Malloy's site

Malloy's *site is a former bridewell (police station). We see the Transit driving into the courtyard of the bridewell so that it is out of sight of the roadway. The van parks and the men get out and approach the site hut.*

19   Site hut

Snowy *opens the hut door, and as the men stand at the entrance, we see the interior in shadows. In the shadows furthest from the door is a figure. As the light comes in from the doorway, we see it is* **George***, dressed as he was before, but now he is enveloped in a pair of trousers several ludicrous sizes too big for him.* **Snowy** *opens the door fully, sees his father and says sadly:*

Snowy: Oh no. Not again, dad.

George: Chrissie told me y' were here.

Chrissie: But I didn't tell y' to turn up.

Snowy: [*Entering the hut*] Come 'head, I'll take you back. [**Snowy** *brings* **George** *out*]

George: I'm only across the road, lad, and I mean I'm doin' nothin'. Besides I thought y' might have been short-handed. You know, son.

Chrissie: Course y' did, but we're all right. Come on, we'll take y' back. [*He turns to* **Loggo**] Get a brew on Loggo, will you, we won't be long.

[**Loggo** *and* **Jimmy** *go into the site hut while* **Chrissie** *and* **Snowy** *lead* **George** *away from it*]

20   Malloy's site

We see **George** *with* **Snowy** *and* **Chrissie** *linking him, moving slowly away from the site hut through the archway to the road and the Royal Hospital.*

Snowy: Where did y' get the trousers?

George: I borrowed them, Michael.

Snowy: Off the giant in the next bed?

George: Next bed but one. Those two miserable sods on either side wouldn't lend me theirs. Anyway, I'm getting transferred from here to Walton Hospital. At an undisclosed fee.

Snowy: What are we goin' to do with you, dad?

George: How about giving me a job as a can lad? I could do that as a start.

21   Site hut

The site hut interior reveals the normal dismal site hut/ workman's room. There are a few old chairs, a bench, a few nudes on the wall alongside an architect's drawing, a Calor Gas heater, a small hob and a kettle. The floor is littered with screwed-up chip papers and old newspapers. A bottle of sterilized milk and a few extremely dirty cups stand on the table. The men are sitting on benches. The kettle has just boiled and **Chrissie** *and* **Snowy** *have just returned. As* **Chrissie** *is nearest the kettle he is about to be mother.*

Snowy: Well yeah, there is a bit of work f'plasterers at the moment.

[*He leaves it at that, he waits for the next inevitable question with a certain pride.* **Chrissie** *begins to pour the water from the kettle into the brew can*]

Jimmy: So what are y' doin' here then on fourteen pound a day?

Snowy: I'm blacklisted.

Jimmy: What for?

Snowy: I start strikes.

Loggo: Not a bad reason.

Snowy: And I'm also in the WRP.

Chrissie: [*Winking at the others behind* **Snowy's** *back*]
Didn't they use to have them during the war — y'know, tin
hats an' gas masks an' knock at y' door if y' haven't drawn y'
curtains?

Snowy: The Workers' Revolutionary Party.

Jimmy: Oh aye. I remember them. They were at our factory
gates the day we closed down. Full of brotherly love and
fight the good fight an' all that. We still closed down.

Loggo: Yeah. But Snowy's different, aren't y', Snowy? Not
the same as all those others in that there . . . 'Workers'
Revolutionary Party' . . . Right that, isn't it? Y' the only one
who's workin' class.

Snowy: I can take it y'know, Loggo. I can take it 'cos I
know my beliefs are right. I've been brought up by me dad
to support what's worth supportin' —

Loggo: I didn't know y' dad followed Everton.

Snowy: All I'm saying is, if y' don't fight, if y' know, if . . .
like I mean, it was easy to be a socialist when I was growin'
up in the sixties, an' even f' most of the seventies.
Everyone was a friggin' socialist then. It was fashionable.
But it's not now . . . Everthin's gone sour, everyone's
lockin' the door, turnin' the other cheek, lookin' after
number one. *But now's the time when we should all be
together.* Now's the time when we *need* to be together, 'cos
. . . 'cos well we're not winnin' anymore. *Don't you see that?*
[*He pauses*] Like, that's all I'm sayin'.

Chrissie: [*Gently*] Of course we see it.

Jimmy: And the last thing we need is t'be told about it,
f'Christ's sake.

Chrissie: 'Cos deep down, most us of know it. But y' don't
look that far, not these days. Not when y' scared Snowy.
And when y' scared, unless y' very special, y' think about
y'self — an' yours. Y' think about feedin' the kids, an'

payin' the rent, an' the effect it's havin' on y' tart — an' even what Christmas is going to be like this year. [*He shrugs*] I'm a married man with two kids, an' y'beliefs go right out of the window when y' debtors knock at your door. [*There is a pause*] And what's more I shouldn't be here now. The sniffers've been round our house twice this past fortnight.

Snowy: But y' need the money.

Chrissie: Got it in one.

Snowy: [*Shaking his head*] I know — I need it too.

Jimmy: Is there no chance of a start with Malloy?

Chrissie: Yeah, well, that's what I want to know an' all. I did a couple of days for him last week. Asked him then, but he sort of avoided it. I've only come today so I can ask him again.

Jimmy: Do you know what? I would do anythin' if I thought . . .

Snowy: What did you used to be Jimmy?

Jimmy: I used to be a machine fitter, *an' I still am.*

[**Snowy** *looks embarrassed*]

Snowy: Frig . . . sorry.

Chrissie: He's here now.

[*We see* **Malloy**. **Chrissie** *opens the door and goes*]

Jimmy: What time is it?

Loggo: [*Flashing his watch*] Oh it's about twenty minutes after we should have started work . . .

[**Loggo** *and* **Jimmy** *move towards the doorway*]

Snowy: Hey — *Hey*! Hang about. Look at the state of y' — panickin' just because the boss is here, jumpin' up an' runnin'. Y'll be touchin' y' forelocks next. [*As he talks, he* *picks up his two lengths of rope and approaches the others near the door*] Let's not make it so obvious, hey? Right? Okay, let's go!

[*He races for the door and gets there first. Laughter as they go*]

22 Malloy's site

Malloy *is in wellies and a tweed suit. He is a quietly affluent, overweight Irishman in his late forties. He should give the impression of being able to handle himself. As the lads walk up from the site hut, he glances at his watch, but without threat. The lads approach him.*

Malloy: One short then are we?

Loggo: Well y' know what it's like. First sign of spring an' all the boys are off to Spain — I mean, after all it's a shame to let the villas go to waste.

Malloy: [*Grinning*] And who are you when you're out?

Loggo: I am *the* brickie. That's how I served my time. It was some time ago but . . .

Chrissie: We did have another brickie but he got a proper job.

[**Snowy** *puts the ropes on his shoulder*]

Malloy: Well. That's good to hear — anyway . . . see y've brought your ropes, Snowy? [*He laughs to himself*] But I don't think they'll come looking for you here, though.

Snowy: This used to be a bridewell, didn't it?

[**Malloy** *nods*]

Snowy: It's not goin' to be a police station again, is it — 'cos y'know, I do have certain moral objections to working . . .?

Malloy: Nah; it's not going to be that. But you could say it was another growth industry. One of the few. Okay, I can leave you on your own now, can't I?

Snowy: [*Turning back*] I'll need someone to mix for me every so often.

Malloy: Kenny'll do that.

Chrissie: [*To* **Snowy**] Kenny won't, but Chrissie might.

[**Snowy** *grins and moves back into the yard to go upstairs with his ropes. He will go to the room he is plastering first*]

Malloy: You're not a brickie, are you, by any chance?

[**Jimmy** *hesitates slightly, then shakes his head*]

Jimmy: Sorry.

Malloy: Don't worry. There's still some landscapin' needs doing . . . that patch over there. Flatten the hump out, pick out all the half sets and rubble and that should . . . that should . . .

[**Malloy** *has just seen* **Yosser** *and his* **children**. **Yosser** *is walking down from a low hill towards them, through the mud, with his three* **children** *in tow. He is walking with the air of a man with total confidence in his own destiny. He appears to know where he is going, even if no one else does*]

Chrissie: [*To* **Loggo**, *quietly*] Look what's coming.

Loggo: Oh frig.

[*They turn away.* **Yosser** *arrives.* **Loggo** *and* **Chrissie** *are looking at him. Only* **Jimmy** *is looking at* **Malloy**, *who is looking at* **Yosser**]

Yosser: [*Smiling, speaking rapidly*] Gizza job, go on, gizzit, go 'head.

Malloy: A job? [*He looks at* **Yosser's children**]

Yosser: Yeah, gizzit, go on. I know you've got one, Arthur told me, go on, gizzit.

Malloy: Now? Today? Well what about the . . . [*He points at the kids*]

Yosser: Oh yeah. Oh aye, yeah. Oh too right, yeah. [*He takes his coat off*] I'm ready.

Malloy: I only need a brickie.

Yosser: Yis, that's me. I'm a brickie. I can lay bricks.

[*We see* **Loggo** *and* **Chrissie** *look at each other*]

Malloy: Well there's er . . . there's . . . that small wall runnin' parallel with the one that he's going to be workin' on.

[**Yosser** *grabs* **Loggo's** *tool bag and is already on his way*]

Malloy: I'll see how you . . . how you make out on . . . [*He is talking to himself. He looks at* **Yosser** *then at the others*] . . . trial basis . . . Do you know him?

Loggo: We used to.

[**Loggo** *walks away towards the two parallel walls.* **Jimmy** *goes towards the rubble-strewn landscape.* **Malloy** *turns away from* **Chrissie** *in the archway and goes towards his car which is parked just around the corner of the building.* **Chrissie** *walks with him*]

Chrissie: . . . How's the new site going, Mr Malloy?

Malloy: Fine, just fine.

[*As* **Malloy** *speaks, we see the first length of rope drop to the ground, right in front of them. They both look up.* **Snowy** *grins down at them, before he pops his head back in. They carry on walking and talking*]

Chrissie: Y' busy then are y'?

Malloy: [*Glancing at him*] Not really, not for the time of the year. And not after the winter we had.

Chrissie: Y' never know, though, we might have a good summer.

Malloy: Still die off once the bad weather comes back. Always does.

Chrissie: I was just wonderin', Mr Malloy.

[*They have reached the car.* **Malloy** *begins to climb in it*]

Malloy: I'm sorry Kenny, but . . .

Chrissie: Chrissie.

Malloy: Yeah, Chrissie. [*He turns the engine over*]

Chrissie: Nevertheless, Mr Malloy, I mean it could be a couple of months before the weather changes.

Malloy: Look, I've really got to dash, y'know how it is.

[*He is moving the car forward, away from the building, towards the side of a three-storey building*]

Chrissie: [*Running with him*] I only want a few words if —

Malloy: I'll be back before dinner, to see how our friend the mad brickie's shapin' up. Speak to me then.

[**Malloy** *spurts away in the car.* **Chrissie** *walks towards the wall of the three-storey section and watches* **Malloy** *go. Another rope cascades down at his side.* **Chrissie** *glances up and sees* **Snowy**]

Snowy: You know the score, Chrissie — there's nothin' down for y'. That's the way it is and that's the way it will be until we —

[**Chrissie** *moves away from the building to look up and glare* *at him, knowing that another piece of politics is on the way down]*

Snowy: Best not to think about it, if it hurts that much.

Chrissie: [*Bitterly*] Yeah, well. We'll see about that.

[**Snowy** *starts to pull in his rope.* **Chrissie** *turns and kicks out at a bag of masonry cement. The bag rips and spurts.* **Chrissie** *walks away]*

23   Snowy's room

We see the room where **Snowy** *is plastering. One door leads to a corridor. Two windows face out towards the parallel walls. Each window is large enough for a man to climb through.* **Snowy's** *rope is attached to and wrapped around a radiator, and then to the window frame, before dropping out of the window.* **Snowy** *is plastering feverishly, whistling. He has the appearance and energy of a little man doing a big job, and doing it very well.* **Chrissie** *is in the centre of the room, standing by the board full of plaster he has just mixed for* **Snowy.** *He walks to the window and wipes his hands.*

Snowy: [*Whistling, looks around as he works*] Thanks, Chrissie.

[*No reaction*]

Snowy: Y' all right?

[**Chrissie** *nods and walks to the centre of the room*]

Snowy: I'll probably need another mix in a few minutes.

Chrissie: [*Still without turning*] You'll be lucky. It's nearly dinnertime now.

Snowy: It's not, is it? Doesn't time fly when y' havin' fun.

[*He laughs and looks at* **Chrissie**. *No reaction again. Then* **Snowy** *talks as he continues to work*]

Snowy: I love doin' this, y' know.

Chrissie: Yeah, I've noticed.

Snowy: I'd plaster f' nothing if me principles'd let me — know what I mean?

Chrissie: Not off-hand, Snowy, no.

Snowy: Y'know, doin' somethin' y' good at — there's nothin' like it. Standin' there in the mornin' facin' four empty walls — an' then goin' home at night with the plaster all dry and smooth — an' the bit y've just done all wet an' shinin' . . . That's why I don't mind workin' on me own, if the truth be told, 'cos if there's one thing I can't stand, it's workin' with someone who hasn't got no pride . . . An' funny enough, they're the kind that never want to come out on strike. No pride *and* no principles.

[**Chrissie** *continues to stare out of the window*]

Snowy: Like some of the sods who've renovated this place. Have y' seen it — it's shoddy already — half the wood's warped, there's a fall in the floor and a leak on the landin'. Nothin'll last here — except the building itself, and the plaster on the walls . . . Y' wanna see somethin'? [*Walks to the centre, stops and looks at* **Chrissie**] Hey Chrissie — come here.

Chrissie: [*Turning to* **Snowy**] Do I have to?

[**Chrissie** *looks at* **Snowy**, *shrugs and half-grins.* **Snowy** *walks to the door*]

Snowy: No, I want to show you something. It won't take long. [*He tests the plaster on the walls*] An' that'll hold for a while.

24   Malloy's site

Jimmy Johnson *is 'landscaping'. He is being helped by*
Yosser's eldest boy *as they pick out the most obvious half sets
and big stones. They have their backs turned to where they are
piling the stones.*

Jimmy: Hey. You can come again, kidder. Keep this up an'
I might just increase your non-taxable allowance to ten p.
an hour. [*He smiles*] You can't drive a JCB by any chance
can you?

[*Suddenly we hear the thud of stone against bucket. They
turn back with a handful of bricks and stones each, and look
towards where they have piled the stones and bricks already
gathered. They see* **Yosser's youngest child** *busy throwing
them all over the place again with gay abandon.* **Jimmy**
sags visibly, and begins to walk over]

Jimmy: What do you think you're doing you little . . . do you
think I'm carryin' these bricks round for the good of my
health? Come on, get them up!

[*As he walks over, we see in the foreground* **Loggo** *and*
Yosser *crouched over their respective walls. But we cannot
make out clearly the quality of their walls*]

Loggo: Eh Yosser . . . Yosser . . . Yosser . . . y' can't leave
gaps like that.

Yosser: It's for ventilation.

[**Loggo** *sighs*]

25   Corridor of third floor

Chrissie *and* **Snowy** *are walking along the corridor.*

Snowy: You see . . .

[**Snowy** *touches the tiles.* **Chrissie** *looks at* **Snowy** *and then at the tiles on the wall*]

Chrissie: It's a tile, Snowy. Lots of tiles. Brown ones.

Snowy: Yeah, I know, I know, nothin' special. Just beautifully made and precision laid a hundred years ago — and still like new. Apart from those that've been cracked to buggery by the idiot who put the new banister up.

[*The rope is hanging out attached to a window frame and the banister, running down the steps leading to the cells.* **Snowy** *touches the tiles again, and the finish.* **Chrissie** *looks at him as he walks out to the landing*]

Chrissie: Is that it? Can I go now?

[*They lift the rope on the landing and walk under*]

Snowy: But don't y'see —

[**Chrissie** *turns away, without insult, and moves towards the door leading onto the flat roof*]

26   Flat roof, Malloy's site

They walk across the roof, back towards where **Snowy** *was plastering.*

Snowy: We're all capable of work like that. Craftsmanship doesn't die out in people, Chrissie. We can all do good jobs, but we're not allowed to. I don't get jobs just because of me politics, y'know.

[**Chrissie** *glances at him*]

Snowy: There's times when I'm not taken on because I'm too good. And because I'm so good, and I do the job proper, I refuse to skimp on the stuff and I'm slower than the bosses want me to be. And then I'm not a profit margin anymore, I'm a liability.

Chrissie: [*Gently, as he puts his arm round* **Snowy**] Do y' ever lose any work because y' talk too much?

Snowy: [*With disarming sincerity*] All right. But listen Chrissie, I'm tellin' you, an' I mean it, don't give in, 'cos if y' give in, y' dead. An' I'm only tellin' y' 'cos I can see the signs.

[**Chrissie** *hugs him like a brother and pushes him towards the door*]

Chrissie: Get in.

[*They go inside the doorway*]

27   Snowy's room

Chrissie *and* **Snowy** *enter the room. While* **Snowy** *looks at his wall,* **Chrissie** *goes to the window and looks out.* **Snowy** *admires the wall he is plastering and the wall opposite the fireplace.*

Snowy: [*Lightly*] Oh hey. Would you look at that? Just look at that. Sometimes, y' know ... [*Almost shyly*] ... Sometimes I'm so proud of what I've done, I put me name on the bottom right-hand corner of the wall ... 'Snowy Malone, 1982'. [*He pauses*] Y'know, Chrissie, thinkin' about it, the job with Malloy ...

Chrissie: *I know.* And I wasn't thinkin' about it just then.

Snowy: Oh ... Still bad down there?

Chrissie: Bad? That's a compliment.

[**Chrissie** *looks at* **Snowy** *and indicates out of the window.* **Snowy** *comes forward and looks out*]

28   Malloy's site

Snowy *and* **Chrissie** *are looking out at* **Yosser** *at his wall, which leads out from the building, no more than two-thirds of a metre in height. The wall meanders from the string line, bricks stick out at odd angles, there is the occasional 'ventilation' gap between bricks, and the cement sticks out from between the bricks. It is, however, a long wall and* **Yosser** *is maniacally making it longer by the second.* **Loggo** *is going along straight and steady on his wall leading from the building, providing a perfect contrast. We also see* **Yosser's** **daughter** *handing him each brick to put into the wall as he goes wildly on. We hear* **Chrissie** *and* **Snowy** *as we see these sights.*

Chrissie: He's off his cake, Snowy. Every time I've seen him since he was with us in Middlesbrough he's just got . . . worse. An' the stories y' hear.

Snowy: Been to see me dad, y'know. Yeah, just turned up one night, sat there with him for nearly an hour, starin' at me dad. Nurse had to ask him to go in the end. When he started cryin'.

29   Snowy's room

Chrissie *and* **Snowy** *are still at the window.*

Chrissie: When who started cryin'?

Snowy: Yosser.

Chrissie: Kinnell . . .

   [*There is a pause*]

Snowy: Y'd better tell him about that.

Chrissie: I already have done. So's Loggo.

Snowy: Y'll have to tell him again, then.

Chrissie: For all the good it'll do. It's like talkin' to a brick wall.

[*He smiles slightly as he realizes what he has said*]

30   Malloy's site

Yosser *carries a spadeful of cement.* **Chrissie** *runs after him. We see the brick wall. We see* **Yosser** *slamming another brick, neither into line nor place. He is bent over, back turned, covered in sand and cement.* **Chrisse** *and* **Loggo** *are alongside him.*

Chrissie: But ... but Yosser, y' don't know what y' doin'. [*No answer*] He'll go spare when he comes back. [*No answer*] Yosser! [*No answer*]

Loggo: Look! Tell y' what, Yos, you work the hod for a while hey, I'll lay the bricks, work a tandem.

[*There is still no answer.* **Chrissie** *looks at the brickwork in despair. He bends onto his haunches.* **Chrissie** *stops* **Yosser** *and points out one of his worst efforts*]

Chrissie: Look Yos, that one's not even —

Yosser: Leave my wall alone.

[*He knocks* **Chrissie's** *hand away with the trowel, stares at* **Chrissie** *and then smiles, wild and warm, before throwing another brick into the wall.* **Chrissie** *gives up, stands up and moves away*]

Chrissie: Come on ... it's dinnertime.

[*As* **Loggo** *and* **Chrissie** *move away and* **Yosser** *goes too, a green Marina van goes past the site on the road above, slightly slower than would be expected. It comes to a halt further along the road*]

31   Road outside Malloy's site

The green Marina van stops almost out of sight of the site.
Moss *is now driving, while* **Lawton** *is the passenger.*

Moss: It's a Mercedes, Leslie. I'm no connoisseur, but I
know a Mercedes when I see one.

Lawton: [*Looking down at the file on his knee*] All I'm saying
is —

Moss: You saw him in it yourself at his other site.

Lawton: All I'm sayin' is that it says here it's a green 'T'-reg
Ford Granada. Obviously he must have changed his car.

Moss: No manners have they, some people? Y' would've
thought he'd have had the decency to let us know.

[*They turn to see a boy go by.* **Yosser's eldest lad** *scampers
past them with a parcel of chips, and goes down towards the
site.* **Lawton** *contemplates reacting to* **Moss's** *sarcasm, but
thinks better of it.* **Moss** *looks up, nudges* **Lawton** *and
indicates as he sees the Mercedes followed by a council
wagon go past towards the site entrance.* **Moss** *smiles and
starts to unpack his lunch*]

Lawton: . . . Still, when you think about it, it's a good job we
had to take that other van back.

[**Moss** *stares dolefully at him for a second or so*]

Moss: Aye . . . That's what your superiors are for — to keep
you completely in the dark. Particularly our delightful boss
— living proof of the folly of female emancipation. Knowin'
her, she wouldn't have told us what was goin' to
happen.

Lawton: It wouldn't be the first time, Donald.

Moss: Don't I know it. Do you know I followed a bloke to
court one morning last month and sat there and watched

while he went to the dock and pleaded guilty to the
offences I was still following him for? [*He looks at* **Lawton**]
I'd been on sick leave when they pulled him in, but nobody
thought to let me know when I came back.

[*He turns right around, to look back through the window
down towards the building site. The Mercedes and the
council wagon pull up in front of the bridewell*]

Lawton: [*He turns*] Well, at least *something*'s happening.
Won't be long now . . . He's got a nerve though, hasn't he,
this Malloy character?

Moss: You mean having lads here? I'll say.

[**Moss** *smiles and then laughs*]

32 Malloy's site

By the entrance leading into the inner yard, **Malloy** *is getting
out of his car which is parked on the corner to give access to the
wagon.* **Malloy** *only has eyes for the wall which he is walking
towards, staring.*

Council worker: Where's the sign goin', feller?

Malloy: . . . What er, oh yeah . . . up there, over the . . .
entrance.

[**Malloy** *walks around the brickwork, and stops with his
hand over his mouth. He looks again, still unable to believe
it. We hear the* **council worker**, *talking to his driver*]

Council worker: Take the wagon in the yard, Phil, and
stand on the back to put it up.

[**Malloy** *glances up at them as they move the wagon into the
yard, so that only the very tail of the wagon is sticking out. He
finally manages to drag himself away from the freewheeling
brickwork and moves towards the site hut, inside the
yard*]

33   Site hut

Inside the site hut, all the men, except **Yosser***, have got some kind of carry-out. A brew is on.* **Snowy** *is starting a joke.* **Yosser** *is sitting away from the others on the floor against the far wall with his* **kids** *and chips. He is sharing the chips out.*

Snowy: . . . I'm havin' terrible trouble sleepin', y'know. It's the dole that does it, though, isn't it? Went to the doctor's last week, told him straight — 'I'm on the dole, doctor, an' I can't sleep'. So fair enough, he told me to take these pills of a night before I went to bed — but I told him goin' to sleep at night wasn't the trouble. So he suggested that when I woke up in the early hours of the mornin', I take one so that I can get me head down again. But I told him that wasn't no trouble neither, so he got a bit ratty with me then, and asked me when it was I couldn't sleep. An' I told him —

[Everyone except **Yosser** *joins in on the punchline. Quietly and almost lethargically]*

All: 'It's the afternoons.'

Snowy: Ah, y've heard it . . .

*[***Malloy** *enters. The lads look up and then away. They move to let* **Malloy** *through.* **Malloy** *makes his way towards* **Yosser***, stands over him and the* **kids** *and then speaks quietly]*

Malloy: You do that wall?

Yosser: *[Looking up as he claws chips into his mouth]* What wall?

Malloy: The wall I asked y' to do.

Yosser: Yeah, what about it? *[More chips]*

Malloy: Come and take a look at it.

Yosser: I've seen it. [*He laughs*] Once you've seen one wall, y've seen them all. [*He laughs again, and looks at the others*]

Malloy: Not this one. This is special.

Yosser: Good hey? [*He looks around again*]

Malloy: Come and see it again. It's well worth seeing twice. [*He turns away and goes towards the door, then stops and looks back*] Now.

Yosser: Don't tell me what to do. Nobody tells me what to do.

[*But* **Yosser** *stands up and follows* **Malloy***, stomps past* **Chrissie** *and out of the door, ignoring* **Chrissie's** *speech*]

Chrissie: Take it easy, eh, Yosser? I want a word with Malloy after . . .

[**Yosser** *goes out, followed by his* **kids**]

Loggo: Well, Chrissie. Y'can always have a cosy little chat while y' walkin' him over to Casualty . . . [**Loggo** *gets up as he talks and goes to follow* **Malloy** *and* **Yosser**]

[**Chrissie,** **Jimmy** *and* **Snowy** *follow him out of the hut*]

34   Malloy's site

Yosser *is standing by the wall with* **Malloy***. The* **kids** *are a few yards away.* **Snowy,** **Loggo,** **Chrissie** *and* **Jimmy** *are leaning against the wall by the wagon. They watch from afar. The* **council men** *are on top of the back of the wagon drilling holes in the brickwork to support the sign as this goes on.*

Malloy: But what were you doing, man?

Yosser: I was doin' my best.

Malloy: Your best? That can't be your best — that's a disgrace. [*He prods at the wall with his toe*]

Yosser: [*Quietly*] Leave my wall alone.

Malloy: But look at it.

Yosser: Last for ever, that.

Malloy: [*Laughing at him*] I know one thing — you're not a brickie.

Yosser: I am.

Malloy: You're not. Y' can't be — not if that's your best.

Yosser: I've laid bricks before. Anyone can lay bricks.

Malloy: Listen son, the last time you laid bricks was when you had a Lego set. [*He reaches for his inside pocket for his wallet to pay* **Yosser** *off as* **Yosser** *leans back to butt him*] You're no good to me.

[**Yosser** *butts him and lays him flat and over the wall. The lads come forward.* **Malloy** *gets up, puts his fists up and tries to hit* **Yosser**. **Yosser** *grabs his fist, and speaks sanely and soberly*]

Yosser: I wouldn't do that if I were you. 'Cos if y' do, I'll kill y'.

[*As they face each other, the two* **council men** *stop and look from the top of their wagon*]

Malloy: Go on, clear off — you're sacked.

Yosser: [*Laughing*] *Me* — sacked? [*Laughs again*] How can y' sack someone who's on the dole? [*Still laughing, he walks to the others. His* **children** *follow him*] He's sacked me, boys, he's sacked a man who doesn't even work for him. [*He laughs*] I'll tell y' somethin' — he'll have trouble findin' me P45.

[*He walks off, kicks his wall over and strides away confidently as the* **kids** *run after him.* **Chrissie** *watches him go*]

35 Site hut

Inside the hut, **Malloy** *is sitting on a chair slightly away from the table and the others. His nose has stopped bleeding but is puffed up.* **Loggo** *and* **Jimmy** *are reading their papers,* **Chrissie** *and* **Snowy** *just finishing off their cups of tea. Silence.*

Snowy: . . . Want another cup of tea?

Malloy: No, no, I can hardly finish this one. Anyway, I've got to go. [*He stands up and looks at them*] And so have you. [*Tries to smile as they look up at him*] Back to work.

[*He waits till they make a move towards the doorway.* **Chrissie** *doesn't stand up.* **Snowy** *watches him, tries to catch his eye.* **Chrissie** *looks away.* **Snowy** *talks to* **Chrissie**]

Snowy: How are you fixed for some more mixin'? Won't take a minute.

Chrissie: An' I won't be a minute.

[**Chrissie** *stays where he is.* **Snowy** *goes and closes the door.* **Malloy** *sits. Both speak together*]

Malloy: If y' —

Chrissie: I was —

Malloy: Go on.

Chrissie: No, no. You.

Malloy: [*Sits down*] Well, I've got nothing to say. It was you wanted to speak to me.

Chrissie: Yeah, well I was … I'm not happy at the way things are now, Mr Malloy, fourteen pound a day and …

Malloy: In y' hand.

Chrissie: Yeah I know, it's all well an' good but it's not legal an' things are bad for me down the dole, an' what I'm sayin' is I want a job. I want a proper job. This is no use to me.

Malloy: Isn't it more use than no job at all?

Chrissie: You don't want to take me on?

Malloy: It's not a question of that.

Chrissie: I know I'm losing money asking you this, but I'd rather be legit on a lot less. *I wanna be a working man again.* I wanna come home at night with dirt on me hands and not have to hide it from anybody.

Malloy: If you would just listen to me for a minute, Kenny —

Chrissie: You don't want to take me on? Right, fine.

[**Chrissie** *gets up and starts packing his stuff into his bag. He collects his paper and tools*]

Malloy: If I took you on, what would happen the weeks when there was no work, when the winter comes again, when I'd have to find your weekly wage so you could play cards, drink tea and piss in the snow? What do you want me to do — take you on for a few months and then lay you off when there's frost on the ground, like the big firms do? Hey? What do you want, promises or the truth, Kenny?

Chrissie: [*He stops what he is doing*] I wouldn't mind me real name. [*He has his anorak on*]

Malloy: Yeah. Chrissie.

Chrissie: That's right, Chrissie. Y' can remember it when I'm gone.

[**Malloy** *gets up and goes to the back of the hut*]

Malloy: You're not listening to a word I'm saying. Look, this is the building game, this is Britain in 1982. It's . . just . . . not . . . worth . . . my while.

[**Chrissie** *heads for the door*]

Malloy: Where are you going?

Chrissie: Home. [*He is now at the door*]

Malloy: [*Calmly*] Can any of the others drive?

Chrissie: No. [*He opens the door, and goes out followed by* **Malloy**]

Malloy: What about the van?

Chrissie: Snowy can handle a moped. Sometimes.

Malloy: [*Deliberately. Flatly*] But what am I goin' to do?

Chrissie: Don't ask me. I don't work for you. Remember?

Malloy: [*Friendly*] Okay, don't worry, I'll find someone. [*He goes for his wallet again*] Here, here's a five f'—

Chrissie: Frig off, Malloy, I don't need charity. Give it to Oxfam. [*He goes to walk off, but stops*] I used t'be soft, y' know, noted for it. But not anymore. I've had it up to here.

[**Chrissie** *indicates his forehead*]

36   Road outside Malloy's site

Moss *and* **Lawton** *are in the green Marina.* **Lawton** *is playing with a Rubik Cube.* **Moss** *is cleaning his glasses. He looks in the mirror and turns to look out as two similar vans come quickly towards the back of their van, both tooting and flashing their lights as they approach.* **Moss** *sits up, turns the ignition on, revs up and throws the van expertly into first gear.* **Lawton** *is still jerked forward however.*

Moss: Sods, they're going to beat us to it. Put that bloody thing away!

Lawton: Has something upset you?

[*They approach the site*]

37   Malloy's site

The **council workmen** *are packing up their ladder. We hear laughter.*

Loggo: Jimmy, I don't believe it.

Jimmy: Hang on, where's Chrissie?

[**Chrissie** *appears through the gap between the wall and the wagon.* **Loggo** *sees* **Chrissie**, *goes towards him and grabs hold of him.* **Loggo** *pulls* **Chrissie** *away from the entrance*]

Loggo: Come here, Chrissie, come on over here . . .

Chrissie: What for?

Loggo: Never you mind.

Chrissie: Oh hey.

Loggo: No, y'll like this.

[**Loggo** *positions* **Chrissie** *with his back turned to the sign above the entrance, a few yards away from it.* **Loggo** *goes behind* **Chrissie**, *puts his hands over* **Chrissie's** *eyes and turns him around as he talks*]

Loggo: Now turn around.

Chrissie: I'm not in the mood, Loggo.

Loggo: Y' will be. Now think hard, what would y' say this is?

Chrissie: Wha'?

Loggo: What do you reckon this buildin' is going to be, eh? This former cop-shop.

Chrissie: I don't know, do I?

Loggo: Well have one guess.

Chrissie: Oh look. Stop friggin' about.

Loggo: Do you give in then?

Chrissie: Yeah, yeah, yeah. I give in.

Loggo: [*Imitating a fanfare*] Der der der der! der der der der! der der der der der! Can you believe it! Look!

[**Loggo** *takes his hands away.* **Chrissie** *is standing in front of the newly erected sign. And we see for the first time that the sign indicates that the building is going to be an unemployment office*]

Loggo: Can you believe that? Can you believe that?

[**Chrissie** *looks at* **Loggo** *and* **Jimmy**. *He grins and giggles. All three rapidly begin to roar with laughter*]

[**Malloy** *is standing by his car, watching, laughing*]

38 Snowy's room

Snowy *is still in the room that he is plastering. He is on his haunches by the bottom right-hand corner of the wall he has just completed. He is putting his name and the year in tiny writing in the corner with a pocket screwdriver. He hears the laughter from the others coming through the window. They are still out of view.*

Loggo: Snowy'll do his bleedin' nut when he sees that.

Chrissie: Get him down here.

Loggo: He'll love this.

[**Snowy** *stops and goes towards the window. He looks down and sees the lads, plus* **Malloy** *just starting his three-point turn*]

Chrissie: Snowy!

Loggo: Snowy, hey, come 'head, come here!

39   Malloy's site

From the outside we see **Snowy** *looking down.*

Snowy: What's the matter?

Loggo: [*Still sniggering*] Come here and we'll show y'. Come 'head.

[*We see* **Snowy** *turn away from the window*]

40   Malloy's site

We see the following events. The three green vans turn into the site at some speed, aiming to get past the building and block the men's escape onto the main road and up the low hill or towards the hospital. **Malloy** *is doing a three-point turn.* **Loggo** *spots the vans arriving and grabs* **Chrissie**, *and the pair of them grab* **Jimmy** *and shout towards the building. They start to run towards the roadway where the green Marina was.* **Malloy** *drives up behind. However, the first van rams straight into the council wagon as it reverses happily out of the entrance to the yard. And the second van hits the back of the first one, and the green van slithers and skids sideways into the second van. For a split second we see* **Lawton** *smirking at* **Moss**, *as they both hold their heads.* **Lawton** *and* **Moss** *attempt to climb out of their battered van.* **Loggo**, **Jimmy** *and* **Chrissie** *run up towards the roadway, but they see another van parked up there,* *with two men waiting for them. The fraud men chase them back towards the bridewell. They shout to* **Snowy**.

Loggo/Chrissie: Sniffers, Snowy! Sniffers!

[**Snowy** *appears at the window.* **Malloy** *arrives and tells them to climb in the car*]

41   Window, seen from outside

Snowy *is at the window. He looks out.*

42   Window, looking outwards

Malloy *arrives in his car. He screams out.*

Malloy: Get in. Get in.

[**Jimmy** *and* **Loggo** *and* **Chrissie** *approach him. They have no option*]

43   Window, from outside

Snowy *looks out of the window as he grabs the rope. He sees a couple of the fraud section men holding the other end.* **Snowy** *turns wildly away from the rope and the window. He runs out of the room and into the corridor, but turns back, grabs his trowel, and then runs out again.*

44   Malloy's site

The Mercedes screams round the corner of the bridewell. **Moss** *is watching the car. It skids round the corner then continues.*

45   Roof outside Snowy's room

Malloy *and the others are bouncing down the road beneath where* **Snowy** *has his rope. As they come towards the window and the rope we see one more van swinging onto the site, blocking the way.* **Snowy** *comes out of the door onto the roof and runs to the railings. He looks down.* **Malloy** *screams the Mercedes into reverse back towards the men now running towards him.* **Snowy** *is hurtling across the flat roof between the room he has plastered and the corridor where he has his second rope. As he runs into the building two fraud men run across the adjacent rooftop and climb over the railings.*

46   Corridor and stairs to window

Snowy *is banging into the corridor. He looks behind himself as he reaches his rope and sees two fraud men entering the corridor. He looks down the stairs where he sees* **Lawton** *coming up towards him.* **Snowy** *grabs hold of the rope, swings out of the window, and starts to go down the rope.* [*The following action is seen in slow motion*] **Snowy** *is still in vision as the banister gives way. The window frame comes apart and he falls.*

47   Malloy's site

Snowy *is falling.* **Malloy's** *car is now going forward, and* **Snowy's** *body drops right in front of it. The car skids to a halt and the four men inside jump out and go to the front of the car.* **Loggo** *takes one look and backs away fast and leans on a wall. The fraud men watch from their top window.* **Jimmy** *turns away. We see the fraud men approach in the green van.*

Jimmy: Here they come.

Chrissie: Yeah, well, get goin'. [*He shoves* **Jimmy**] Well go on — y' don't know him — an' anyway, what can y' do? He's dead.

[**Jimmy** *turns and races down the road towards the car park, followed by a fraud man.* **Malloy** *turns to* **Chrissie**]

Malloy: [*Leaning on the Mercedes*] Look, tell them I just started you all, that I asked for your P45s, and that you were bringing them in tomorrow. Please. This could ruin me. Please listen to me. I'll give you a job, I will, *I'll make it worth your while.*

[**Moss** *has walked up behind them.* **Chrissie** *grabs* **Malloy** *by the lapels and pushes him. He falls to the ground by the car.* **Chrissie** *bends down by* **Snowy**'s *body and looks at his blood ebbing away into the dirt.* **Moss** *starts reading the standard caution to* **Malloy**]

Moss: By the powers invested in me as an officer of the Department of Employment, I am obliged to inform you that I am empowered to apprehend you from unlawfully employing certain persons who are claiming full unemployment benefit. Do you wish to say anything? You are not obliged to say anything, but if you do what you say will be taken down and may be used in evidence.

48   Malloy's site

Jimmy Johnson *is running away through the building site, hotly pursued by a fraud man.* **Jimmy Johnson** *runs into the entrance to the Royal Hospital and picks up a bunch of flowers to hide his face behind. The action freezes as the sound of an ambulance siren is heard.*

Eileen O'Brien as Freda and Tom Georgeson as Dixie Dean in Moonlighter

Moonlighter

First shown on BBC2 on 17 October 1982

Characters

Dixie Dean
Freda Dean, his wife
Kevin Dean, his eldest son, unemployed

At the Department of Employment
   Assistant Manager
   Dixie's clerk (female)
   Jackie Mills

At the Docks
   Haich, a docker
   Scotty, another docker
   Marley, a security supervisor
   Third docker
   Fourth docker
   The Laughing Cavalier, a 'security guard'

Malloy, a building contractor
Marie
Danny Dean, Dixie's second son
Janet Dean, his daugher
Stephen Dean, his eleven-year-old son
Chrissie Todd

Loggo Lomond
George Malone
Voice on telephone

Moonlighter

---

1   Department of Employment building

The opening shot establishes the Department of Employment building.

2   Department of Employment building

Dixie *is asleep on a bench. He wakes. Someone arrives and sits down behind the grille. She is a* **counter-clerk***, and has* **Dixie's** *claim in her hand.*

Clerk: [*Calling out*] Mr Dean. Mr Dean.

Dixie: [*Looking round as he gets up*] About time too.

Clerk: Pardon?

Dixie: I've been waiting here f' forty minutes. If I'd known I would've brought a packed lunch.

Clerk: Well, the quicker we get this over with, the quicker you can go.

   [*The* **clerk** *looks down at the claim. Then at* **Dixie** *again*]

Clerk: You're not in a hurry to go anywhere are you?

Dixie: Nah, I don't have to be back at work for ages yet. [*He smiles*]

Clerk: [*Easily*] I take it that was meant to be a joke?

Dixie: Yeah, a sick one.

Clerk: Right ... Name?

Dixie: Thomas Ralph Dean.

Clerk: Age?

Dixie: Forty-four.

Clerk: Date of birth?

Dixie: Twenty-third of the third, nineteen thirty-eight.

Clerk: Where do you reside?

Dixie: Forty-seven Maryvale, the Hilltree Estate.

Clerk: How long have you resided there?

Dixie: Fourteen years.

Clerk: Are you resident at any other address?

Dixie: The Penthouse Suite at the Holiday Inn.

Clerk: Are you resident at any other address?

Dixie: No.

Clerk: Have you done any work since your last signing on?

Dixie: No.

Clerk: Is your wife employed in any capacity?

Dixie: No.

Clerk: Are any other members of your family employed in any capacity?

Dixie: No.

Clerk: Do you intend to start work before your next signature?

Dixie: No.

Clerk: Are you sure that you are not employed in any capacity?

Dixie: Yes.

Clerk: Thank you, Mr Dean.

Dixie: It's been a privilege and an honour.

[*He goes*]

3   Public lavatory cubicle

We see **Dixie** *during the following night's work. He is a security guard for 'Southgate Security' on the docks. However, we see him dressed in a normal, everyday winter manner until the end of the scene. He is sitting in a cubicle in a public toilet, on the toilet seat but with his trousers still on. He is nervous, smoking and looking at his watch as he waits. After a few seconds we hear someone enter the next toilet.* **Dixie** *looks at the wall between them. The toilet paper that has been thrust into a hole in the wooden dividing wall is being pushed into* **Dixie**'s *side of the toilet.* **Dixie** *looks towards the small whittled spy hole. A small roll of five-pound notes is slid through and falls to the floor. More toilet paper is thrust into the hole. We hear the other man going out of the toilet and off.* **Dixie** *looks again at the hole before picking up the money. When he unfolds the money, he doesn't seem at all happy.* **Dixie** *comes out of the toilet and takes his hat out of his mac pocket. He puts it on. In the mirror we see it is a security guard's hat.*

4   Public lavatory in docks

Dixie *comes out of the toilet. It is early evening, going or just gone dark. The toilets are on the edge of the docks. A small cargo vessel is in the background about forty yards away, but otherwise the area is deserted.* **Dixie** *makes his way towards the vessel. As he approaches it, we see a Ford Cortina approach from the opposite direction, picking up speed as it goes. The*

driver puts his headlights on full beam, deliberately catching
Dixie *in their glare. He backs away, but the car reaches him
and stops.* **Dixie** *approaches it. The car has 'Southgate
Security' signwritten on it. The driver winds down the window
and looks out at* **Dixie**. *We see the driver. He is* **Marley**, *the
security man in charge of that area of the docks for Southgate
Security. He is near retirement age, big, heavy-set, a former
policeman. He is in full security uniform and still has the
demeanour of a policeman. Everyone is suspect.*

Marley: You're early.

Dixie: [*He leans in*] Er. Yeah. [*Defensively*] Well. The same
bus was late last night. Y' can't tell these days.

Marley: That's true enough.

[*There is an awkward pause as* **Dixie** *doesn't quite know
what to do. He hesitates about going*]

Marley: I expect you want your money?

Dixie: Wouldn't go amiss.

Marley: Come and sit inside the car.

[**Dixie** *does so.* **Marley** *pulls a plain white envelope out of
his pocket.* **Dixie** *takes it*]

Dixie: Oh, ta.

[*He puts it in the same inside top pocket as the other money,
struggling slightly as he puts it in. He then uses his other
hand to move the five-pound notes aside. He glances up at*
Marley, *who watches and notices without expression, and
waits till* **Dixie** *has finished*]

Marley: Aren't you goin' to count it?

Dixie: No. It's all right. I trust y'.

Marley: Some security guard you must be then.

Dixie: No, well, I mean . . . Oh, well, all right then.

[**Dixie** *goes gingerly to take the envelope out of his pocket, but* **Marley** *waves his hand, indicating* **Dixie** *not to bother.* **Marley** *drives to the gangway*]

Marley: Should sail the day after tomorrow. So they say.

Dixie: What happens then?

Marley: There'll be others. The port isn't quite dead yet. Despite the efforts of all concerned.

Dixie: I mean, y'know . . .

Marley: Expect the firm'll keep you busy for the next few weeks, till the end of the contract. And then it's 'Goodnight Vienna'.

[*He stops his car, turns the engine off and gets out.* **Dixie** *gets out too*]

Dixie: What d'you mean?

Marley: [*Lighting a cheroot*] Haven't you heard?

Dixie: No. [*He shakes his head*]

Marley: We've lost the security contract with the shippin' line. The fourth in eighteen months and the last one on these docks.

Dixie: You're joking. Why's that?

Marley: Could it be because we're not security guards, walking around sayin', 'It's all right, I trust y''?

Dixie: Hey now. Hang on. I mean, I've only been here a week.

Marley: [*Ignoring him*] Who cares? Nobody else seems to these days, why the soddin' hell should I? [*He sighs*] At least I've still got my police pension.

Dixie: Are you going too?

Marley: They've told me already. Anyway you're no longer early and the Laughing Cavalier's up there waiting for y'. Have fun and y'never know y'might even find the dockers turning up for a game of cards later. Got to do somethin' to pass the time.

[**Marley** *gets into his car and drives off as* **Dixie** *goes up the gangway and along the deck*]

5   Cargo ship

Dixie *is 'between decks' in the hold of the boat. He is approaching another 'security guard' with the same lack of uniform, who is sitting on some sacks and a crate, facing the cargo in the hold, which is over one-third full. The* **guard** *has a limp and a large scar across the side of his face. Singing 'Nobody's Child'.* **Dixie** *walks towards him.*

Dixie: All right. [*No answer*] Y' can go now.

The Laughing Cavalier: I was goin' to.

[*The* **Cavalier** *stands up. Picks up his duffle bag*]

Dixie: That's what I like about this job — the comradeship.

[*His remark appears to have no effect, as* **The Laughing Cavalier** *walks a couple of paces away. But then he turns back*]

The Laughing Cavalier: Y'haven't been here very long, have y'?

Dixie: Nah, it just seems like a lifetime.

The Laughing Cavalier: Y'll soon learn — y' don't have friends in this job. The only friends y' likely to have are those that want favours. And they're no kind of friends at all.

[*He walks away through the hatchway without waiting for a reply. As he goes,* **two dockers** *saunter towards him wearing donkey jackets, jeans and carpet slippers or plimsolls. Both are carrying dockers' hooks. They pass* **The Laughing Cavalier**]

Scotty: There he goes, the ship's rat.

Haich: Now leave him alone, Scotty. Show some respect for the dead.

[**Dixie** *sits on a crate. The* **two dockers** *approach* **Dixie** *facing the hold. They sit at either side of him. They too look down*]

Haich: All right, it's Dixie isn't it? I'm Haich. [**Dixie** *nods*] On all night again are you? [**Dixie** *nods again*] Nice night for it. [*No answer. Pause*] Be on again tomorrow night will y'? [**Dixie** *nods*] Be an even better night for it. [*He grins at* **Dixie**, *then looks across at the* **second docker**] Have a look for his tongue, Scotty, I think he's lost it. [**Scotty** *lifts up a packing case and some sacks*] Like it here do y', Dixie? [**Dixie** *shrugs*] Could be worse, eh.

Dixie: Yeah. Suppose so.

Haich: It's okay, Scotty. Y' can stop lookin'. He's found it again. [*Back to* **Dixie**] Nice boat, isn't it?

Dixie: It's all right, as boats go.

Haich: Oh, it's more than that. It's even more than nice. I'd even go as far as to say it had personality . . . character.

Scotty: Charm even. [*He drifts away towards the hold*]

Haich: Oh aye, yeah. Charm as well. Especially charm.

[*Three more dockers arrive, wearing plimsolls and carrying dockers' hooks*]

Haich: [*Getting up*] All right lads, I was just telling Dixie here, it's a superb boat this.

[*The* **third** *and* **fourth dockers** *nod*]

Haich: Do you know why?

Dixie: No.

Haich: It hasn't got containers.

[**Haich** *moves to the edge of the hold. We see* **Scotty** *rooting about.* **Haich** *shouts down*]

Haich: Try over there by that Nigerian dried milk, Scotty.

[**Dixie** *hears* **Scotty** *rooting about in the hold. He gets up and joins the dockers at the edge of the hold*]

Dixie: What . . . what's y' mate up to down there?

[*They look down*]

Haich: Oh he's a strange lad is Scotty. He always thinks of things in terms of a football match. [*He leans forward and looks down*] It's his philosophy in life. I expect he's tryin' t'break through the defence. Bit of a Kenny Dalglish is Scotty. Y've got t' keep y'eye on him all the time.

Dixie: Look, y'do know what I'm supposed t' be doin' here, don't y'?

Haich: Yeah, you're the goalkeeper.

Haich: Here they are Haich. [*He starts to open the crate*]

Haich: And it looks as though y've just conceded a goal. [*He moves back*]

Scotty: Right, what sizes d' y' want?

[*He starts to throw boots*]

Haich: Nines f'me, Scotty.

Third docker: Got any elevens?

Scotty: Elevens coming up.

Fourth docker: Eights for me and two pairs of sevens for me lads.

[*The dockers are still surrounding* **Dixie**. *There is something stylized, rehearsed about their movements.* **Dixie** *stares at them, then at the* **second docker**, *who throws one pair of boots up, soon followed by others*]

Scotty: What about you, pal?

Dixie: Who?

Haich: [*Quietly*] You.

Dixie: What?

Haich: What size d' you take? [*Pushing him*] Put your foot there, put it alongside mine ... [*Putting his foot by* **Dixie's**]

Dixie: Now look, lads ...

Haich: Nines. Scotty. Get him nines. Take y' shoes off, Dixie — y' could do with a new pair.

Dixie: Are you pullin' my pisser?

Haich: Not unless y' keep it in y' shoe pal. Here y' are. Sit down.

Dixie: No.

Haich: Come 'head.

[**Haich** *is pushing* **Dixie** *back towards the crates. The others gather round*]

Dixie: [*Sitting*] Ah no, you're not on.

Haich: Why not?

[**Dixie** *holds the boot up*]

Dixie: I can't wear these.

Haich: Y've got the wrong size, Scotty.

Dixie: But I'm a security guard.

Haich:　We all have a cross to bear.

Dixie:　I'm here to stop you.

[*The* **third** *and* **fourth dockers** *lean over him holding their dockers' hooks close to* **Dixie's** *face and then* **Haich** *leans over him*]

Haich:　. . . And are you gonna stop us?

Dixie:　. . . I don't want any trouble, y' know. This . . . isn't me real job.

Haich:　Course it's not. You're on the dole. Aren't y'?

[**Dixie** *nods*]

Dixie:　Yeah.

Haich:　You're not alone, blue. There's only Marley and his Ford Cortina that's real down here, the rest of the crowd're the same as you. Don't worry about it.

[*The* **dockers** *all bend down to put their new boots on*]

Dixie:　Look. I just don't want no trouble like, you know.

Haich:　Y' won't get any, go 'head.

[**Scotty** *arrives*]

Dixie:　But won't anybody say nothing?

Scotty:　Yeah, they'll go friggin' mad in South Africa.

Haich:　And by the time they arrive there, this boat'll've been to three other ports. [*He laughs*] They'll be lucky to have any boots left.

[*The* **dockers** *are still putting their boots on*]

Scotty:　So there y' are.

Haich:　Safe and sound.

Scotty:　So long as you don't tell anyone, now Dixie.

Haich:　'Cos that wouldn't be very nice, would it?

Scotty: We wouldn't like you anymore.

Haich: Just when we were gettin' to know y'.

Scotty: It'd be a crying shame.

Haich: We'd be upset.

Scotty: As well as angry.

Haich: But you'd be the one who was hurt.

[**Dixie** *looks at them*]

Scotty: So there.

Haich: See. Come on. Scotty, stand on me boots, will you, scuff 'em up a bit.

[**Haich** *and* **Scotty** *stand on each other's boots. The others follow suit. They start dancing and singing 'These boots were made for walking'.* **Dixie** *looks down at his own boots.* **Dockers** *sing: 'One of these days these boots are going to walk all over you'*]

6   Docks

It is daylight, the following morning. **Dixie** *is on his way home. He walks along the sea-wall.*

7   George's road

Funeral cars and wreaths are lined up outside **George's** *house. There are also private cars and an ambulance with two ambulancemen standing nearby, smoking. Four or five people come out of the house and get into cars. Amongst them are* **Loggo** *and* **Chrissie**. **Chrissie** *is dressed formally in black. They stop and* **Loggo** *lights up a cigarette.* **Dixie** *approaches. All three are flat and uneasy throughout.*

Chrissie: All right, Dixie?

Loggo: Dix.

Dixie: Snowy?

Chrissie: Yeah.

Dixie: I heard.

Chrissie: You were nearly there. That was the morning I called for you and y' —

Dixie: I know. [*He looks towards the* **Malones'** *front door*] George?

Chrissie: Don't ask, Dix. [*A pause*]

Loggo: How're you keepin' anyway? Long time no see.

[*He offers* **Dixie** *a cigarette but it is a waste of time*]

Dixie: Yeah, the last time was Middlesbrough, Loggo. Remember?

[*They look at each other.* **Loggo** *and* **Chrissie** *give* **Dixie** *the victory of looking away*]

Dixie: I'm doing all right, I'm gettin' by.

Chrissie: [*Looking down*] Goin' for long walks?

Dixie: Bus never came.

Chrissie: I hear it's nights. [**Dixie** *nods*] Still signin' on?

Dixie: No option.

Chrissie: Yeah, well. Be careful.

Dixie: [*Looking away*] In more ways than one.

[**Loggo** *turns and sees* **Snowy's** *coffin being brought out by the funeral attendants and family as* **Dixie** *finishes speaking. The ambulancemen approach.* **Loggo** *stubs out his cigarette and stands aside.* **George** *comes out of the house, supported lightly by two men of his age, his brothers, perhaps. A small family group follows.* **George** *is near to but not in tears. We almost hear him before we see him*]

George: I'm goin' in the car, I'm not goin' there in that, tell them I'm goin' in the car, will y'.

[*The two men release their grip on him, and he walks slowly but firmly towards the first car as the coffin is slid into the hearse. The other mourners get in the cars.* **Loggo**, **Chrissie** *and* **Dixie** *are looking down*]

Loggo: I'm off. I can't stand requiems and cemeteries.

[**Loggo** *walks quickly away, head down, the way* **Dixie** *has come.* **Chrisse** *and* **Dixie** *walk to funeral car*]

Chrissie: See y', Dix.

[**Dixie** *looks up*]

Chrissie: Hey if you're around our way . . . well, you know, y' know where I live.

Dixie: [*Walking off*] What d' you want me to do — 'make friends'?

[**Dixie** *turns and walks off.* **Chrissie** *hesitates a second and then gets into one of the cars. The doors on the funeral cars close, and the back door of the hearse is slammed shut*]

8 Dixie's hall

Two letters are lying on the floor by the door in **Dixie**'*s hall. One of them is in a brown government envelope. We hear* **Dixie** *open the front door and see his new boots. He sees the letters, picks them up and moves towards the living room.*

9 Dixie's living room

Dixie'*s living room is part of a three-up and two-down new council house. It is very tidy.* **Dixie**'*s middle son,* **Danny**, *aged* *nearly sixteen, is lying on the sofa reading a magazine and listening to music.*

10   Hall

Dixie *walks through the hall.*

11   Living room

Danny, *in pyjama top, jeans and bare feet, is eating toast. When he hears his dad coming, he shoves the plate of toast under a cushion. He tries to look sick and hold his stomach.* **Dixie** *enters and is about to open the letters when he sees* **Danny** *who groans.*

Dixie: What are you doin' here, Danny?

Danny: I'm not ...

Dixie: Get dressed an' get to school, go on.

Danny: But I've had these ... [*He clutches his stomach*]

Dixie: Where's y' mother?

Danny: She's ... [*He points towards the back kitchen wall*]

Dixie: Are Kevin an' Janet here?

Danny: They're still in ... [*He points upstairs*]

Dixie: Is Stephen at home as well?

Danny: He's ... [*He points through the front windows of the house*]

   [**Dixie** *goes to the door and shouts*]

Dixie: Freda, Freda!

12 Kitchen

Freda *looks out of the kitchen. She is an attractive vague redhead in her early forties. She does her very best.*

13 Living Room

Dixie *turns back to* **Danny**.

Dixie: How many times have I told you about trying it on with y' mother?

Danny: But I've got a sore stomach, dad, honest.

Dixie: Y'll have a sore arse if you're not off it an' up those stairs. Now go on, git!

[**Danny** *gets up quickly, half expecting a clout as he goes past* **Dixie**. *He gets one. They go out towards* **Freda** *in the hall*]

14 Hall; at bottom of stairs

Dixie: Hey!

Danny: What now? [*He stops*]

Dixie: What chances have y' got of leavin' school with any qualifications if y' never there in the first place?

Danny: [*With contempt*] Qualifications . . .

Dixie: What's wrong with qualifications?

Danny: Y' need nuclear physics t'be a binman these days, dad.

[**Danny** *goes up the stairs.* **Dixie** *points his finger as if to argue, then stops. He looks at the letters again as he goes into the hallway, and then to the kitchen door.* **Dixie** *kisses* **Freda**]

Dixie: I'm going to bed, girl. That seems t'be the fashion in this house.

[**Dixie** *opens the electricity bill, then starts to open the other letter as* **Freda** *follows him upstairs*]

Freda: They don't mean any harm, Tommy, they just don't listen to me . . .

Dixie: Oh, for God's sake! *What are they doin'?*

Freda: It's cheek mainly, an' stayin' in bed, but . . .

[*At the top of the stairs* **Dixie** *hands the letter to* **Freda**. **Janet** *comes out of the bathroom.* ('Morning dad, mum') *She goes between them and enters her room.* **Dixie** *opens the door. She closes it on him*]

15   Dixie's landing and boys' bedroom

Freda *has just realized that* **Dixie** *is referring to the letter. They have reached the landing facing the boy's bedroom.* **Danny** *and young* **Stephen** *share bunk beds.* **Kevin** *has a bed of his own.* **Dixie** *leans on the top banisters and flicks the letter at* **Freda**. *Then he looks into the boys' room and sees* **Danny** *putting his school uniform onto his bed. He also sees* **Kevin** *flat out and asleep.*

Dixie: Look at him, just look at him — soddin' Sleepin' Beauty . . .

[**Dixie** *goes into the bedroom*]

Freda: But what does it mean?

Dixie: It means I'm not goin' to bed.

[**Dixie** *goes to the bathroom.* **Freda** *follows*]

Freda: I thought you went there yesterday though.

Dixie: Too true I did.

[*He is washing his face*]

Freda: What do they want you for again?

Dixie: Maybe they've found me a job.

[*He goes into their bedroom to change*]

Freda: [*Sitting down*] That'd be nice.

16   Department of Employment building

Dixie *is back at his previous position at the counter of the DoE. He is looking at the* **clerk** *from his previous test check.*

Dixie: What do you mean, you don't know nothin' about it — what's this, then? [*He puts the paper up at the grille; she jumps*] A chain letter? Look at it — *look!* [*He pushes it under*]

Clerk: But I've already looked, Mr Dean, and I've ...

Dixie: Get me someone worth talkin' to — come on, come on.

Clerk: But my ...

Dixie: *Get someone.*

Clerk: I'm trying to tell you, this letter wasn't sent by my department.

Dixie: *Well who sent it then?*

[*The* **assistant manager** *of the fraud section appears as if he had been waiting for this cue. He is in his mid-thirties. He wears a leather jacket and lots of contempt. He has* **Dixie's** *claim in his hand*]

Assistant: Mr Dean?

[**Dixie** *nods*]

Dixie: Yes.

Assistant: Thought it might be. We sent the letter, Mr Dean.

[*He walks out from behind the grille.* **Dixie** *joins him*]

Dixie: And who are you when you're out?

Assistant: The employment section.

[*He motions to* **Dixie** *to go into the interview room. They do and he closes door. The* **assistant manager** *goes through and summons the* **clerk**]

Assistant: Jean — would you mind?

[*She gets up and joins him in the interview room*]

Assistant: Thank you.

[*She sits.* **Dixie** *sits reluctantly*]

Dixie: Yeah, all right, but before we start, this is the second day runnin', an' the third time in a month I've been called in — now what's the score?

Assistant: Routine. Merely administrative routine.

[*Walks round* **Dixie**]

Dixie: I can use big words as well, y'know. [*He leans forward with confidence and enunciates carefully*] 'Elastoplast'.

[*The* **assistant manager** *doesn't flicker.* **Dixie** *leans back sourly. The* **assistant manager** *sits*]

Clerk: Name?

Dixie: Y'already know it. Y've used it y'self.

Clerk: Name?

Dixie: And so did he.

Clerk: Name?

Dixie: Are y' sure this isn't a trick question?

[*As the* **clerk** *goes to ask his name again,* **Dixie** *joins in, then answers the question. He continues in the same manner*]

Clerk: Name?

Dixie: Thomas Ralph Dean.

Clerk & Dixie: Age?

Dixie: Forty-four.

Clerk & Dixie: Date of birth?

Dixie: Twenty-third of the third, nineteen thirty-eight.

Clerk & Dixie: Where do you reside?

Dixie: Forty-seven Maryvale Street, the Hilltree Estate.

Clerk & Dixie: How long have you resided there?

Dixie: Fourteen years.

[*The* **clerk** *changes the order of the questions as she and* **Dixie** *speak together*]

Clerk: Are you employed in any capacity?

Dixie: Are you resident at — ah, you changed the order of the questions! That's not fair!

Clerk: Mr Dean —

Dixie: [*He points*] You're a cheat.

Assistant: Mr Dean, you must realize that nothing can be gained from treating our enquiries in this manner. It quite obviously helps neither you nor I, and furthermore, you're hardly original in your approach. Quite frankly, it has been some years now since I have found even the slightest glimmer of amusement in antics of this nature. [*He nods at the* **clerk** *to carry on*]

Clerk: Are you employed in any capacity?

Dixie: [*To* **assistant**] Do you practise makin' speeches?

Clerk: *Are you employed in any capacity?*

Dixie: Nah, I never have the time, do I? I'm always too busy comin' here. It costs 32 pence on the bus, too.

Assistant: In most cases these test checks are picked out at random, Mr Dean, if that's any help to you.

Dixie: The bus fare'd be more help.

[*Then the* **clerk** *continues and* **Dixie** *looks away*]

Clerk: Have you done —

Clerk & Dixie: — any work since you last signed?

Dixie: No.

Clerk: Is your wife —

Clerk & Dixie: — employed in any capacity?

Dixie: No. Are any other members of your family employed in any capacity? No. Do you keep budgerigars in the bathroom? No.

Assistant: Are you sure about the last question you were asked, Mr Dean?

Dixie: Yeah, they'd shit all over the place wouldn't they? [*But he's not quite so confident*] Which one?

Assistant: The one with regard to your wife.

Dixie: Yeah.

Assistant: Not being employed in any capacity.

Dixie: That's what I said, wasn't it.

Assistant: Nothing at all?

Dixie: *No.*

Assistant: Not even a couple of hours a day, cleaning? Something like that? Helping her friends run a little . . . business?

Dixie: I said no before, didn't I.

Assistant: Well. Perhaps she hasn't told you. Women can be forgetful, you know.

Dixie: *Look, what the hell is this*?

Assistant: I've finished now, Mr Dean. Thank you, You can go.

[*The* **counter-clerk** *looks at the* **assistant manager**, *then at her papers.* **Dixie** *gets up and goes without comment. The* **assistant** *makes a brief note in* **Dixie's** *claim as he talks. The* **clerk** *packs up and gets up to go*]

Assistant: So he wants to play funny buggers, does he . . . Do me a favour, would you — go over to my section and find out who we've got floating this afternoon. See who finds it funny then . . .

Clerk: If you don't mind me asking, there's nothing about his wife in there.

Assistant: [*As he finishes writing*] That's correct.

Clerk: How did you know?

Assistant: I didn't [*He grins and puts the claim away in his briefcase, then takes out another one as he talks*] We . . . er . . . got some information the day before yesterday, from someone who's proved to be reliable in the past, indicating that half his road are claiming for their wives while their wives are working. So I've got everyone in that road who's signing on coming in this afternoon. Put the fear of God into them if nothing else. [*Looks down at the next claim*] Stephen Jefferies please . . .

[*She goes out*]

17   Dixie's living room

Dixie's *daughter,* **Janet**, *is in the room with her dressing gown on, dancing.* **Dixie** *and* **Freda** *enter,* **Dixie** *first.*

Dixie: He knew. I'm telling you, he knew.

[*He stubs out his cigarette*]

Freda: But who told him?

Dixie: I didn't like to ask.

Freda: Oh.

Dixie: Someone's blown you up, Freda. [*He takes his coat off*]

Freda: But who'd do a thing like that?

Dixie: More people than y' realize. Come on, Janet, will y'.

[**Freda** *takes* **Dixie's** *coat out*]

Janet: What?

Dixie: The time!

[*He goes*]

18   Kitchen

Dixie *joins* **Freda** *in the kitchen.*

Freda: Does that mean I'll have to stop?

[*She makes the coffee*]

Dixie: What do you think?

Freda: It's only a pound an hour, three afternoons a week.

Dixie: Y'may as well be sellin' state secrets to the Russians, it's all the same t'them.

Freda: You won't be able to go to the docks, Tommy, if they're checkin' up.

Dixie: I've got to go tonight. [*He goes to the table*]

Freda: Surely you could give it a miss for one night.

Dixie: I can't.

[*He sits down.* **Freda** *joins him*]

Freda: Don't get upset, Tommy, y'know it —

Dixie: Janet!

[**Dixie** *jumps up*]

19   Living room

Dixie *storms into the living room and pushes* **Janet** *onto the sofa.*

Dixie: It's gone twelve o'clock.

Janet: So?

[**Dixie** *turns the record off*]

Dixie: So get upstairs and get some clothes on!

Janet: [*She gets up*] But what for?

Dixie: Don't 'what for' me, girl, just get up there and do it.

[*She goes towards the hall. He follows*]

20   Hall

Janet: There's no need t'take it out on me.

[**Janet** *begins to go up the stairs with* **Dixie** *following as he speaks to* **Freda**]

Dixie: What did she say?

Freda: [*Lying*] I never heard her.

Dixie: [*To* **Janet**] What did you say then?

[**Janet** *leans over from the landing*]

Janet: Nothin'. An' anyway our Kevin's still in bed.

[**Dixie** *looks at* **Freda**]

Freda: I have shouted him.

Dixie: Some job he'll get, lyin' in bed all day.

[**Dixie** *runs up the stairs.* **Freda** *waits at the bottom*]

Freda: Er no, don't go up, Tommy, I'll get him now.

[**Dixie** *rounds the top of the stairs, goes out of view and shouts*]

Dixie: Kevin!

21   The boys' bedroom

Kevin *is fast asleep in his single bed. We hear* **Dixie** *bouncing up the stairs. The door opens.* **Dixie** *goes to the side of the bed.*

Dixie: Kevin. Come on, get up.

[**Kevin** *mumbles as he is wakened*]

Dixie: D'you know what time it is?

Kevin: Er ... No. [*He yawns*]

Dixie: It's quarter past twelve.

Kevin: Is that all?

Dixie: I want you to get up.

Kevin: It's too early, Dad. Anyway, what is there to get up for?

[**Dixie** *grabs the duvet and hurls it away from the bed*]

Dixie: Get up!

Kevin: What d'you do that for?

Dixie: Because y' a bloody disgrace, Kevin. You're not even tryin' any more.

Kevin: Leave off, will y', just leave off.

Dixie: Get y' clothes on an' get out an' look f' work.

Kevin: There is none.

[*They are both shouting*]

Dixie: There is none when y' lyin' in bed.

Kevin: An' there's none when I'm walkin' up an' down the industrial estate neither! You know that — you've been there with me as well. I've been left school two-and-a-half years. I've been out of work for two of them, and I've never so much as had a bastard interview. [**Kevin** *punches his bed*] So don't give me no crap about lyin' in bed.

[**Kevin** *gets off the bed, grabs the duvet, lies down and covers himself.* **Dixie** *seems set to explode further, but he can't find the words. He tries for a second or two and then goes out. We hold for a second or two, as* **Dixie** *slams the door shut and then* **Danny** *begins to crawl out from under the bottom bunk where he has been hiding. He is still in his pyjama top and jeans. The phone begins to ring downstairs*]

22 Dixie's hall

There is a pay-phone to one side of the bottom of the stairs. It is ringing. **Dixie** *is at the bottom of the stairs. He picks the phone up.*

Dixie: Yeah?

Voice: [*Pleasant, insidious*] Dixie Dean?

Dixie: That's right.

Voice: Now you don't know me, but you got a little bonus off a friend of mine last night, a fifty pound bonus just for starters, and all I'm doing, Dixie, is giving you a little reminder that if you want the rest of the bonus and you want to keep your features you'll be a good little boy tonight.

[*The phone goes dead immediately.* **Dixie** *looks at the receiver, again at a loss for words*]

23   Dixie's hall

Freda *has her coat in her hands. As* **Dixie** *returns, we see her putting it on.*

Freda: Who was that?

Dixie: Oh, er, no one, nothin'. [*He looks at her*] What are you doin'?

Freda: I've got to tell the other girls, I can't just leave them.

Dixie: Y' jokin' aren't y'?

Freda: They'll all be waitin' for me.

Dixie: An' that's just what they want.

Freda: Oh. Er . . . Who?

Dixie: You go see other girls, right? Bad man with binoculars see you, right? Bad man follows you, sees you meet other girls in mo-mo car — right?

[**Freda** *starts to undo her coat*]

Freda: All right Tommy.

Dixie: Bad man follows nice girls, sees nice girls puttin' leaflets through letter boxes for pound notes, no questions asked, make bad man with binoculars happy, bad man rides into town, forms posse, nice girls get captured.

[**Dixie** *turns into the lounge.* **Freda** *speaks with dignity as she takes her coat off*]

Freda: I'm not completely soft, y'know. You don't have to talk to me like that. Before you went on the docks, we needed the money I got with the girls, it was the only money we had coming in.

Dixie: I know, I know.

Freda: Your Giro doesn't go far, Tommy. Not with —

[**Dixie** *screams his reply*]

Dixie: I know!

[*He goes into the lounge.* **Freda** *follows*]

24 Lounge

Dixie *goes to the window, looks out, and pauses.* **Dixie** *turns away from the lace curtains, to the easy chair.* **Freda** *comes to the door.*

Freda: D' y' want some dinner?

Dixie: Nah, I've got to get some sleep. [*He sits down*] And listen, if anyone comes sniffin' around asking questions, wantin' to come in, I don't care who they say they are, you don't tell them nothin', an' you don't let them in.

[**Dixie** *takes his new boots off.* **Freda** *walks in, sits down*]

Freda: Surely they wouldn't come here? [**Dixie** *looks at her sadly*] They're not allowed t' come in are they, an' just . . .

Dixie: Y' don't know much about the ways of the world, do y'?

Freda: But that's terrible. What am I going to say?

Dixie: [*Picking up his boots*] You don't say nothing. You don't even open the door.

Freda: Where d'y' get the boots?

Dixie: [*He puts them down*] They fell off a boat.

[*He puts his hand into his jacket pocket, takes out the envelope containing his wages. He throws the envelope in her lap. Then pulls out the other money, peels off three five-pound notes and hands her the rest. She looks at the roll of fivers, bewildered*]

Freda: Who gave y' all this?

Dixie: A man in a toilet. [**Dixie** *picks the boots up and stands*]

Freda: Are you feelin' all right, Tommy?

Dixie: Never better.

[*He goes out and she follows him into the hall*]

25   Hall

Freda: You're not in any trouble, are y'?

Dixie: You ask more questions than the dole, you do.

Freda: But Tommy . . .

Dixie: Get y'self somethin'. Somethin' for y'self.

[*He starts to go up the stairs.* **Freda** *stares at the envelope and the money. She is becoming scared. She goes into the kitchen*]

26 Kitchen

Freda *is in the kitchen.* **Dixie** *and* **Danny** *are out of view but we hear them.*

Dixie: Hey Danny, what the friggin' hell do you think you're doing?

Danny: Me mam said I could . . . [*There is a loud smack*] Ow! Array, dad.

27 Dixie's kitchen

Freda *comes to the window and looks out. There is a red Ford Escort parked a few yards away but all we can see, and only vaguely, are a blonde woman and a man.* **Freda** *sees the car and hides the money in a cake tin. An old battered Mini arrives with three women inside of the same age and class as* **Freda.** **Freda** *reaches for the blind as one of them gets out and comes up the path to knock on the door.* **Freda,** *looking worried, closes the blind and waits. The woman then looks through the front window but* **Freda** *closes a second blind. The woman goes back to the door, and starts knocking.*

28 Dixie's hallway

Freda *has crept from the kitchen and crawled round to the front door. We see* **Freda** *up against the door. She has lifted the letterbox lid — two-thirds of the way up the door — and is talking through it. She doesn't see any comedy in the situation at all. All we can see of the other woman,* **Marie,** *are her eyes, and when she talks, her mouth.*

Freda: Stop knockin' will y'.

Marie: But we've been waitin' ages for y'.

Freda: I can't come out, Marie.

Marie: Is one of the kids ill?

Freda: No, it's them — they're after me.

Marie: They're what?

Freda: They're after me.

Marie: Who are?

Freda: The whatsits — the dole.

Marie: Since when?

Freda: They had Tommy in this mornin', questionin' him about me. They know what's goin' on.

Marie: [*After a pause*] What is going on?

Freda: The job — the leaflet thingies.

Marie: Ah, we've been doin' it for years, Freda. They'd have caught us by now. Come on, get y' coat on.

Freda: I can't. It's not safe, I might be followed.

Marie: We're givin' away threepence off cornflakes, not robbin' banks, now are y' comin' or what?

Freda: I daren't. Y'd better go, Marie, they could be watchin' us right now.

Marie: Don't worry, they'll just think I'm kissin' y' door.

Freda: [*She turns in*] Go 'way. Please go away.

Marie: . . . Bloody hell, Freda.

[**Marie** *goes.* **Freda** *sits facing out*]

29   Dixie's house

Marie *moves her lips away from the letterbox. Then she walks away towards the gate as a young window cleaner comes up the path with a bucket and ladder.*

Marie: Y' wastin' y' time there, lad.

[He looks at **Marie** *and then carries on. He rings the bell to ask for some water. As he does so, the letterbox lifts up]*

Freda: Go next door. *[He stares at the letterbox]* Go on, if y' want water, go next door. And if you're on the dole, be careful, I'm being followed.

[The letterbox snaps shut. The window cleaner looks around himself, shakes his head and moves quickly away. We see **Marie** *and the others in the car.* **Marie** *has obviously told the others. They are shrieking with laughter as the car goes. We hold on the scene as the Ford Escort begins to follow. Only the driver, the man, is now in the car. The blonde woman,* **Jackie Mills**, *has got out of the car and is crossing to* **Freda**'s *front door]*

30   Dixie's hallway

There is knocking on the door. **Freda** *is at the door of the living room, hidden from the hall.*

Freda: Oh sweet Jesus ... *[She moves towards the coat-rack and hides]* What do y' want?

[We hear a terribly cheerful, confident and cosmetic voice]

Jackie Mills: Hello Mrs Dean.

Freda: Er ... hello.

Jackie Mills: It is Mrs Dean, isn't it? *[***Freda** *goes to open her mouth]* I'm Jackie Mills, your perfume party representative.

Freda: Since when?

Jackie Mills: You've been recommended to us, Mrs Dean.

Freda: It's news to me.

Jackie Mills: Nevertheless, if I could just have a few moments of your time, to have the opportunity to show you the many new and exciting perfumeries and cosmetics in our range, which, if you would permit me to hold a party at your home, you will be allowed to purchase at over thirty percent off retail price, and also enable you to enter our free competition for a weekend in Paris for two!

Freda: No.

Jackie Mills: Please, Mrs Dean, if you could spare the time to see our superb catalogue of —

Freda: Me husband's in bed, I don't want to disturb him.

Jackie Mills: Oh I am sorry, I didn't realize, is he on night work?

[**Freda** *is about to say 'yes', but manages to check herself*]

Freda: ... he's ill. He's ill in bed.

[*Thereupon the phone rings*]

Freda: There's the phone, I'll have to go. Goodbye. Thank you. [*She goes to the phone*]

Jackie Mills: Don't worry about me, Mrs Dean, I can wait a few moments.

[**Freda** *turns to the phone and picks it up*]

Freda: 2033.

[*We hear the man who spoke earlier to Dixie*]

Voice: Now would that be Mrs Dean?

Freda: No, it's the Queen of friggin' Sheba. Now what d' y' want?

Voice: [*As he laughs warmly*] Your husband.

Freda: He's in bed.

Voice: Well, when he gets up, darlin', tell him the man with the bonus rang — tell him I was talkin' to you — and that depending on certain events, we might meet one day, you and I.

[*The phone goes dead.* **Freda** *is out of her depth. She puts down the phone, and then makes for the door*]

Freda: Now look here, I don't want no soddin' perfume, and I don't —

[*We hear* **Malloy's** *voice coming warmly through the door from a position out of* **Freda's** *sight. Then he moves into view*]

Malloy: Hullo Mrs Dean, it's me, Franky Malloy love . . .

31 Dixie's house

We cut to outside the door as **Malloy** *talks.* **Jackie Mills** *is still there. She is a well-dressed attractive blonde in her late twenties, holding a clipboard and carrying a shoulder bag. She does look like a perfume representative.* **Malloy** *looks tired and slightly crumpled, despite the charm and warmth of his voice.*

Malloy: Is Dixie there?

Freda: He's in bed, he's ill.

Malloy: It's nothin' serious is it?

Freda: Yes, no, I don't know.

Malloy: Not workin' then?

Freda: No.

Malloy: Look, can I come in for a minute, I feel a bit of a —

Freda: No.

Malloy: I'm offerin' Dixie some work and some ready —

Freda: Sssssshhhhhhhh!

Malloy: What?

Freda: [*Gabbling*] I'm bein' investigated, Mr Malloy. It's not safe to talk. I'm at risk, and you've been done yourself by the dole, Tommy told me, so go away, just go away. I can't take much more.

[*There is a pause as* **Malloy** *looks at the door, then glances at the girl*]

Malloy: Yeah, all right. But when he gets up, ask him if he'd be interested in a few weeks' work. Tell him I'll give him a ring later, okay . . .

[**Malloy** *turns away.* **Jackie Mills** *speaks to* **Freda** *through the letterbox*]

Jackie Mills: I'll be going now as well, Mrs Dean. I can see it's obviously not an appropriate time. I'll call again. Bye!

[*There is no answer, but then she hasn't waited for one. She catches up with* **Malloy** *as he reaches the garden gate. They walk towards* **Malloy's** *car*]

Jackie Mills: Mr Malloy. My name's Jackie Mills, I'm a perfume representative for . . .

Malloy: Sorry, I don't wear perfume and I don't like parties . . .

[**Jackie Mills** *laughs and then offers him her most alluring smile*]

Jackie Mills: I hope you don't mind me asking, but I take it you're a married man?

[**Malloy** *stops, but then sets off again*]

Malloy: It shows, does it?

Jackie Mills: Not at all, but I wonder if your wife would like to hold a party in your house to display the many new and exciting perfumeries and cosmetics in our range.

[**Malloy** *is getting into his car*]

Malloy: [*With no edge and hardly any interest*] Sorry, y' wastin' your time, love. My wife buys her make-up in bulk.

[*He drives off. Three or four schoolchildren aged about twelve approach from across the road. She watches as* **Malloy** *drives away. She looks between the children to see his registration number. She writes it on her clipboard*]

32   Dixie's hall

Freda *is lighting a cigarette. She is sitting on the floor with her back to the door. We hear another knock on the door.*

Freda: Frig off, whoever you are!

[*Outside is a confused eleven-year-old* **Stephen**]

Stephen: It's only me, Mam.

[*She gets up and lets him in, picks up the ashtray and leaves*]

33   Dixie's bedroom

It is dark inside **Dixie** *and* **Freda's** *bedroom though there are hints of light from behind the curtains.* **Dixie** *is asleep. An alarm goes off, then stops.* **Dixie** *switches on the bedside lamp. He climbs out of bed in his underwear. There are a suitcase and* *a grip on top of a wardrobe, plus the usual double bed, dressing table, chest of drawers.* **Dixie** *slips his trousers on.*

34 Dixie's landing

Dixie *comes out onto the landing fastening his shirt. He begins to go downstairs, but stops and decides to go into the boys' bedroom next to his and* **Freda's** *room. The door is shut. Excellent 12-bar blues is being played on a guitar.*

35 Boys' bedroom

The door is closed. The music stops as **Dixie** *knocks.* **Dixie** *enters and stands by the door.* **Kevin** *is sitting on his bed, leaning back against the wall. He is in his sweat-shirt and underwear, guitar in hand.* **Danny** *is also in the room, reading a football magazine. He looks at* **Dixie** *as he enters and then buries his head in the magazine.* **Dixie** *stands in the doorway.*

Dixie: [*Flatly, finally*] Quarter to six.

Kevin: I'll get dressed in a minute.

[**Kevin** *starts playing again*]

Dixie: Why bother? Another few hours it'll be time for bed again.

Kevin: I'm going out after.

Dixie: Y' stay away from the police this time.

[**Kevin** *nods,* **Dixie** *looks at* **Danny** *who hides behind his magazine*]

Dixie: What are y' goin' to do?

[**Kevin** *stops playing*]

Kevin: Y' mean tonight?

Dixie: No, I don't mean tonight.

Kevin: ... I'll make the rounds again tomorrow. There's a factory at the far end of the estate I haven't been to yet.

Dixie: What about ... What if you was to ... D'you want a job?

[**Kevin** *looks at him coldly*]

Dixie: Yeah. All right. [**Dixie** *closes the door*] What would happen if y' was to leave home? Would y' leave home?

[**Kevin** *nods slightly and* **Dixie** *notices this before looking away. He leans against the wall, then looks at* **Kevin** *again throughout the scene*]

Dixie: It's obvious none of us are helpin' each other. Fightin' never seems to lead anywhere 'cept to another fight. An' y' can still get a job out of town, y'know. Long contracts. The out-of-town-boys.

Kevin: On the blackstuff?

Dixie: Beggars can't be choosers.

Kevin: Can lad and dogsbody.

Dixie: I know it's not what y' want, Kevin. But what I'm doin' these days isn't what I want neither.

Kevin: Y' don't have to tell me. I know that.

[*He smiles at his father. But* **Dixie** *doesn't notice the smile*]

Dixie: If I'd had any sense ... if I'd ... known what was goin' to happen, I wouldn't have done some of the things I have done. To you. I sort of ... made a lot of mistakes with you, son.

[**Kevin** *swallows.* **Dixie** *is looking down.* **Dixie** *opens the door which he is nearly facing anyway. He rushes out and as he exits, the phone goes downstairs. We stay in the room briefly.* **Danny** *lowers his magazine and can hardly constrain his sniggers. He looks over at* **Kevin** *and bursts out laughing.* **Kevin** *promptly throws a football at him. It hits him hard and straight in the face*]

36 Dixie's hall

Freda *and* **Stephen** *are in the kitchen. When the phone rings, she looks out.* **Dixie** *is coming down the stairs. The phone is still ringing out.* **Stephen** *is in the kitchen, spreading a sardine spread butty.* **Freda** *is in quiet fits. She sees* **Dixie** *and crosses out of the kitchen.*

Freda: Oh Christ, Tommy, thank God you're up.

Dixie: Answer the phone, will y'.

Freda: I don't want to.

[*She meets* **Dixie** *on the stairs. He looks at her as he reaches the bottom of the stairs, then picks up the phone. He speaks cautiously. She leans through the stairs*]

Dixie: Yeah?

Malloy: Dixie, hello there — it's Franky Malloy here.

Dixie: Hallo, Malloy. What do you want?

Freda: He's been to the house.

[**Dixie** *puts his hand over her mouth*]

Dixie: And whatever it is, count me out.

Malloy: Dix, it's urgent. It's good money and it's sound.

Dixie: [*Without anger*] Sound — after what's been happenin' to you? Y've just been caught red-handed and Snowy Malone dead an' all. How sound is that?

Malloy: Believe me . . .

Dixie: And they're sniffin' around here and all. There's no chance — we may as well carry banners around town announcin' the time and place.

Malloy: But this one's handsome, the firm isn't in my name, nobody —

Dixie: Yeah, yeah. Thanks for the offer — you've helped me out before — but I'm up to my eyes in shi — [*He looks at* **Freda**] — difficulties already. Sorry.

[*He puts the phone down and crosses to the lounge. She runs after him*].

Freda: There's been other phone calls, Tommy.

37   Docks

Dixie *is running through the warehouse. As he goes, we see the ship's mate watching him. It is the same part of the docks we saw earlier and is night again.* **Marley's** *car is by the side of the gangway, empty, with its sidelights on.* **Dixie** *is running up the gangway and continues along the deck.*

38   Cargo ship; deck

Marley, *who is waiting at the boat rail, lights a cheroot and looks at his watch.* **Dixie** *walks along the deck towards him.*

Marley: Don't tell me, it was the buses.

[**Dixie** *shakes his head*]

Dixie: No, the chauffeur was late.

Marley: I'm sorry to hear that.

Dixie: Yeah, an' the au-pair couldn't find me cap. [*He digs*

the security hat out of his pocket] Y' let the Laughin'
Cavalier go?

[**Marley** *nods*]

Ta.

[**Marley** *seems very relaxed*]

Marley: Keep an eye on the sods tonight, last night in port,
that's when they all start their little tricks.

Dixie: Right. You be around?

Marley: Here and there. [*He misses a beat*] Why?

Dixie: Just wondered, y'know. I mean if they got up to
somethin'.

Marley: There's nothin' worth robbin' on this boat apart
from a few crates of salmon and the odd pair of boots.

[**Dixie** *fights against looking at his feet.* **Marley** *appears not
to notice*]

Marley: Anyway, I thought I might slip back to yours, see
what your au-pair's like.

[*He clicks his teeth*]

Dixie: Ah, y' wouldn't stand a chance, the butler's bagged
off with her.

[*They both grin.* **Marley** *walks away.* **Dixie** *hesitates.*
Marley *is now walking down the gangway.* **Dixie** *runs
along the deck towards him*]

Dixie: Mr Marley! Mr Marley!

[**Dixie** *catches up with* **Marley**]

Dixie: If f' some reason, like, I should need y', where will
y' be?

Marley: They're off-loading precious metals on pier

number three. I'll be there all night, me an' the Dock Police, searchin' dockers' pockets for gold nuggets.

[**Marley** *goes off down the gangway*]

Dixie: Right.

[**Dixie** *watches him go. We watch* **Dixie**. *We see anxiety take over, and how nervous he really is. He turns and walks up the gangway*]

39 Cargo ship; the hold

Dixie *crosses from the right while the dockers cross from the left. They meet in the middle.*

Dixie: All right lads, I'm off now.

Others: Eh?

Dixie: I'm going now.

Haich: [*With genial contempt*] Say that again.

Dixie: I . . . I've just told y' — I was told to disappear.

Haich: Who've you been talkin' to — Paul Daniels?

Scotty: That's a name to conjure with.

[*They laugh*]

Dixie: Look. All I know is that when you lot start doin' whatever it is y' doin' —

Scotty: We were thinkin' of havin' a party.

Haich: An' you're definitely on the invitation list.

Dixie: But I was told to . . . my message was to stay out of the way for an hour or so.

[*The* **dockers** *circle in.* **Haich** *shakes his head*]

Haich: Oh no. No no no no no.

Dixie: No?

Haich: No.

Scotty: No.

Haich: [*To* **Dixie**] You're not goin' nowhere pal. [**Haich** *smiles*]

[**Dixie** *goes to move away. They put their hooks on the wire guard-rails to surround him*]

Dixie: Hey now look, I don't want no part of this.

Haich: Except the money.

Dixie: I'm gettin' paid for not bein' here.

Haich: But I've just told you we're invitin' y' to stay.

Scotty: To the party.

Dixie: That wasn't part of the arrangement. I don't do things like this. I'm not a thief.

Haich: Thief. Thief! Did someone say thief? [*He turns to* **Scotty**] Are you a thief?

Scotty: Not me. Must be you lah. [*Looking at the* **third docker**]

Dixie: It's not my style.

Haich: It is now, pal.

Dixie: All I want t'do is keep me nose clean, keep out of the way an' clear off home.

Haich: Tough.

[**Dixie** *is visibly upset*]

Dixie: Look, my tart's had threatenin' phone calls all bloody day long about this. Now that's not good for me is it?

Haich: But y' see, you bein' here is a sort of . . . a safety valve, you see, because with this job, we don't know who's settin' it up, 'cos it's a mystery this one. It's clever but it's got no trademark. It's not the usual system an' the same bunch of rogues. There's a big question mark about it. And y' see, if we're bein' set up . . . if someone like that bastard Marley is lookin' to go out with a bang, or someone like you, Dix, is lookin' to collect a few medals, we've got to have some insurance.

Scotty: Some cover.

Haich: Against accidents.

Scotty: A kind of limited liability. [*To the others*] Good, hey? Limited liability! [*But no one laughs*]

Haich: And you're all of those, you are Dix. [*But when he talks again, his tone is brutal*] An' listen to me, Mr Clean, if y' thinkin' of lookin' down y' nose at us, let me tell you, the worst robbers on these docks are the so-called security guards — nothin's sacred t' some of your kind. Royal Mail, personal effects, medical supplies, missions of mercy to starvin' countries. I've seen men wearin' caps an' badges rip into all of them an' y' know why — 'cos the likes of you, y' shite. You're nothing. Y' the dregs, dragged here off the dole. Now stand there an' do what y' supposed to do — watch us work.

[*They all file past* **Dixie**. *We stay with* **Dixie** *who doesn't move. We see, before he puts his head down, that he is beginning to weep silently*]

[*We see the following rapid scenes*]

40   Ship's hold

The ship's mate is walking along the edge of the hold. He looks in to see. The **dockers** *are working deep in the bottom of the hold, moving and lifting away any cargo that is in the way of the bonded locker, where the goods of any value are kept. It is a* *compartment of varying size, usually custom-built to the side of the hold and behind steel doors.*

41   Ship — between decks

We see the ship's mate climb down the ladder in his uniform. He arrives between decks. He looks at **Dixie**, *who has his head down. The ship's mate begins to climb further down into the hold.*

42   Ship's hold

The **dockers** *are taking boxes out of the bonded locker. The steel doors to the bonded locker open, and the mate and* **Haich** *walk out of the doorway smiling.* **Haich** *looks skywards out of the hold.*

Haich: There's a van outside loading up now but I just want a word with my mate here. [*He walks across and shouts*]All right up top. Bring the hook across. [*Turns to* **Scotty**] Go upstairs an' keep an eye out, Scotty. Take the toe rag with y'.

[*As the hook moves across* **Haich** *looks towards* **Dixie**. **Scotty** *leaves followed by* **Dixie**. *The dockers start fixing the hook to the crate*]

43   Ship deck/dockside

A van is parked up alongside the ship. Two men are throwing cartons of cigarettes off the crane palette into the van. We hear **Dixie** *and* **Scotty** *before we see them.*

Dixie: Surely a load like that's goin' t' be missed?

Scotty: Oh, it will. But not off this boat. [*We see* **Dixie** *and* **Scotty** *leaning over the side.* **Scotty** *turns to* **Dixie**] The boat that should be carryin' that lot sailed thirty-six hours ago. Our friend the first mate's just been lookin' after them, keepin' them in a safe place. For a favour. And a price. Everyone's got a price, right, all men can be bought, and the incorruptible man has the highest price of all.

Dixie: Shite.

Scotty: No, Swift.

[**Scotty** *crosses to the hold and looks down*]

Scotty: Oh, very crusty, the first mate's gettin' the whisky out. See, I told you we were havin' a party.

[*He goes. When the men finish loading the van it is driven away.* **Dixie** *stays where he is, watching the tail lights of the van disappear.* **Dixie** *turns and looks into the hold. There is indeed a party going on. We see the first mate passing whisky around to a congregation of dockers*]

44   Public lavatory cubicle

Dixie *is in the same cubicle of the toilets as before. We see his boots on the toilet floor. He is in his socks. We hear someone enter the toilet, go past* **Dixie's** *cubicle and enter the next one.* **Dixie** *looks at the hole in the wall. The toilet paper comes out, followed by three separate rolls of ten-pound notes, and then more toilet paper is shoved into place.* **Dixie** *takes the money.* **Dixie** *waits as he hears the other man opening the toilet door. He waits further till the man goes past, then he stands up on the toilet. He looks over the top of the cubicle door to see* **Marley** *walking away from him towards the mirror where he adjusts his hat and walks out of the toilet.* **Dixie** *ducks down.* **Dixie** *turns away and closes his eyes momentarily. Then takes his security hat off and flicks it into the toilet bowl. He flushes the toilet.*

45   Dixie's house/stairs/landing/bedroom

Dixie *walks up the stairs and into the bedroom. It is dark when he enters the bedroom. He crosses to wardrobe. We see* **Freda's** *reflection in the mirror. She is in bed. She makes a startled noise as he moves the case. Then she switches the lamp on. He takes suitcase down.*

Freda: What ... [*Looks at the alarm clock*] You're early, Tommy.

[*He unzips the grip and sits*]

Dixie: Yeah. Well, after I took part in the robbery of half a million cigarettes and got my share of the proceeds, there wasn't much else for me to do. So I decided to come home.

[*He lies back on the bed.* **Freda** *sits up*]

Freda: Don't you think it'd be a good idea to go and see the doctor love? Y've been sort of ... [*She looks at the suitcase*] *Tommy! Where y'goin'* ?

Dixie: Out of me mind. I'll be back in a minute — get my side of the bed warmed up, go on.

[*He gets up and leaves the room. She moves over*]

46   Boys' bedroom

We see the boys' bedroom. **Danny** *and* **Stephen***, in their bunk beds, hear* **Dixie** *open the door.* **Dixie** *enters and goes to* **Kevin's** *bed.* **Kevin** *is fast asleep.* **Dixie** *puts the grip down flat on the floor by the side of* **Kevin's** *bed. He unzips it and throws two rolls of ten-pound notes in. He looks at* **Kevin** *for a second or two, puts the third roll in, then goes.*

47 Dixie's back door

Freda *sees* **Kevin** *off down the path and away. She is crying.*

48 Approach road to M62

Kevin *is standing by the approach road to the M62. He is trying to hitch a lift. The action freezes.*

Michael Angelis as Chrissie and Julie Walters as Angie in
Shop Thy Neighbour

Shop Thy Neighbour

First shown on BBC2 on 24 October 1982

Characters

Chrissie Todd
Angie Todd

At the Department of Employment
  Miss Sutcliffe
  Assistant Manager
  Donald Moss ⎫
  Lawton   ⎬ two fraud section officials
  Jackie Mills, another DoE official

Yosser Hughes
Loggo Logmond
George Malone, Chrissie's uncle
Malloy, a building contractor
Mrs Sutcliffe
Gas man

The children
  Clare Todd
  Justine Todd
  Jason Hughes
  Anne Marie Hughes
  Dustin Hughes

Shop Thy Neighbour

1 Back yard; Chrissie's house

We see the backs of a row of terraced houses one of which is **Chrissie's**. *We finish up in* **Chrissie's** *back yard.* **Chrissie** *and* **Angie** *are out of view but we hear the following dialogue.*

Chrissie: Oh yeah, yeah, yeah. As ever, as bloody ever. You know, forever and ever — the same soddin' things.

Angie: And you know why they're the same soddin' things — because you do nothing about them. They don't go away on their own Chrissie. They don't go away because you lie in bed and mope about the house.

Chrissie: Oh, be quiet and give your arse a rest.

Angie: That's your department.

Chrissie: I said shut up.

Angie: I won't.

Chrissie: Shut up.

Angie: I won't shut up. Why should I shut up? You started it.

Chrissie: Oh yeah. What did I do?

Angie: Nothin'. That's how you started it.

[**Chrissie** *comes out of the back door leading to the yard. He* *slams it shut. The back kitchen door opens again.* **Angie** *looks out. The geese squawk.*]

Angie: I used to slam doors when I was seven!

[*She can't help herself and actually slams the door to close it.* **Chrissie** *half smiles, opens the door and leans on it*]

Chrissie: You haven't changed much have you?

[*He closes the door again. Again the door is open by* **Angie**. *Just a flash*]

Angie: It was the draught.

[*She closes it again*]

Chrissie: [*To the geese*] You can shut up an' all.

[**Chrissie** *half sighs, half grins. He moves further into the yard and picks up a bag of food*]

Chrissie: Here.

[*We see that his yard is full of animals. A pigeon loft, a chicken pen, a ferret's cage, a rabbit's cage and a goose pen. There is a tortoise in the corner. He feeds the lettuce to the rabbit, then glances at the ferret*]

Chrissie: You can die.

[**Chrissie** *looks in the pigeon's cage, and feeds the rabbit. We see the ferret.* **Angie** *is at the window putting on her coat. She opens the door*]

Angie: I'm taking the kids to school.

Chrissie: Yeah, all right.

[**Angie** *points to the animals*]

Angie: I'm glad to see they're having their breakfast.

Chrissie: [*Flatly*] Don't start, Angie.

Angie: Y'can feed y' soddin' animals . . .

[**Chrissie** *is feeding the geese. He holds up a bag of vegetables*]

Chrissie: I robbed these from the bins at the back of the greengrocers.

Angie: Well next time, have a look in the butcher's bins for us.

[*She turns away and closes the door.* **Chrissie** *empties the bag of sprouts over the heads of the geese*]

2   Miss Sutcliffe's living room/kitchen

A gramophone is playing 'This Is My Lovely Day'. We see a dining table. A woman with her back turned is standing and moving away from the table, which is laid out for a now completed breakfast. We see a bowl of wheatmeal cobs, granary bread, a butter dish, an expensive coffee pot and a single used cup and saucer. The centre of the table holds muesli, honey, high-powered marmalade and a splendid bowl of fruit. On the far side of the table another place has been set for breakfast, but not used. And the handsome, late middle-aged manageress of the fraud section, **Miss Sutcliffe,** *crosses to the sink with her plates. She then goes to the mirror, looks, then crosses to the fridge/freezer which is casually well stocked. She takes out a plastic bag full of salad, leaves that on the cupboard surface, then crosses to the inevitably well-stocked wine-rack for a bottle which she slips into the bottom of the fridge. It is as if she does this every day of the week. She goes out into the hall to collect her post. A door opens at the top of the stairs, and we see just a blur of white nightdress as someone scrambles for the bathroom and closes the door. Like a ghost on the run. We hear the click of the bathroom lock. The manageress throws the letters down on a trolley, and looks towards the room that 'the* *ghost' had just come from. The door is open. The manageress approaches it. We see she is in her stocking feet. She enters the room.*

3   Bedroom

The music is much louder in this room. There is a disarranged bed in the room, with the covers on, and a soaking sheet with a rubber underneath. Again as if she does this every day, the manageress takes the wet sheets off the bed, puts them in a wicker basket and jams the lid back on. She crosses to a box of tissues, takes some, wipes her hands and drops the tissues in a bin. She crosses to the gramophone and switches it off. The music stops. She goes.

4   Corridor

The manageress moves towards the main room and the bathroom. We hear the sound of running water. She goes to the bathroom door, listens to the water briefly, then half-heartedly tries the handle. She winces. Her voice when she speaks is resigned.

Miss Sutcliffe: . . . Mother.

[*She knocks on the door*]

Miss Sutcliffe: Come on, Mother. Please.

[*She knocks again. And again*]

Miss Sutcliffe: Mother! Mother you know I need to . . .

[*She looks down suddenly at her bare feet. There is water coming from underneath the door, onto her feet. She jumps back quickly and then comes forward again. She bangs on the door desperately, then tries to barge against it as the water keeps coming*]

Miss Sutcliffe: Mother! Mother! Mother! Mother!

5 Bathroom

Miss Sutcliffe *is out of view but we hear her shouting.*

Miss Sutcliffe: Mother!

[*We hear* **Miss Sutcliffe's** *bangs and attempts to open the door. We see inside the bathroom. The water is running, but straight down the plughole. A very old lady in a nightdress is sitting on the floor pouring water out of a water jug carefully under the door. She starts laughing, an insane cackle*]

6 Corridor

We come back to **Miss Sutcliffe***. She has stopped thumping the door. She puts her head against it, and stands listening to the mad cackle. She is standing in the wet.*

7 Back of Chrissie's house

Chrissie *is sitting on a tea-chest cleaning a double-barrelled shotgun. The back door opens inwards.* **Angie***, still in her coat, comes out. She sits down by him.*

Angie: ... I'm sorry.

Chrissie: It's all right. I'm getting used to it.

[*She looks at him*]

Chrissie: You're giving me nothing but crap all the time these days.

[*She starts to reply and we hear several knocks on the front door.* **Chrissie** *barely registers them. We hear* **Angie** *inside the house, going through the hall to the front door, though she is now out of view*]

Angie: All right, all right ... [*She opens the front door, misses a beat*] Chrissie!

[*He gets up, leaving the gun in the yard*]

8   Back kitchen through to hall

As he enters the house she is already sweeping past him into the back kitchen. She speaks as she crosses him.

Angie: It's your comrades in crime ...

[**Loggo** *and* **Malloy** *enter.* **Malloy** *closes the door. They stand just in the doorway.* **Loggo** *is already shamefaced.* **Chrissie** *slams the door that leads from the hall to the kitchen*]

Chrissie: [*Immediately*] Y' jokin' aren't y'?

Malloy: What do you mean?

Chrissie: Coming here. That's really smart, that is. Did you bring him?

[**Loggo** *nods*]

Chrissie: So that's what friends are for. Thanks Loggo, thanks a lot — now take him away. Far away.

Loggo: Hang on, hang on.

Malloy: Listen Chrissie ...

Chrissie: Are y' sure it's not Kenny or Benny or Arthur or Frank?

Malloy: Chrissie ...

Chrissie: How about Veronica?

Malloy: Oh, look. You're not being —

Chrissie: Look you, plums — me an' him 're in front of the fraud section this mornin' because of you — our Snowy got killed because of you . . .

Malloy: Ah steady on now, that's not . . .

Chrissie: Because of you, I've had my dole stopped, I'm up to here in debt, I can't support my family, my wife's givin' me shite, [*We see* **Angie** *open the kitchen door*] and for all I know I'll be up in court and down the road. Because of you.

Malloy: Y' mean I kidnapped you and made you work for me — third slave to the right on the rowing boat?

Chrissie: All y' had to do, Malloy, was to' stop goosin' me on the side and make an honest man out of me, that's all, y' bastard. Now go on, get out.

[**Chrissie** *goes into the lounge. They follow*]

Loggo: Chrissie . . .

Chrissie: Y' can call me Kenny if y' want, Loggo.

Malloy: Y' being unfair to me. And I've suffered as well. They're makin' me bankrupt. I'll go down before you —

Chrissie: Aaaahhhhhhhhh.

Malloy: And I know y' not listenin' to me. I accept that. But for once, do yourself a favour and . . .

[**Chrissie** *walks to the front door and opens it, waiting for them to leave.* **Chrissie** *turns away*]

Chrissie: I am doin'. I'm ignorin' y'. And remember this, I don't want to see you ever again.

[**Chrissie** *goes out of the lounge back into the hall. They follow*]

Malloy: Chrissie, forty notes a day, in your hand, sound as a pound . . .

[**Chrissie** *goes towards the kitchen*]

Chrissie: [*Loud*] Where did I put me gun, Ange?

Malloy: [*Giving up. He looks outside*] All right, all right, can you get anyone else, Loggo?

Loggo: Yeah, [*Looking away*] I'll try, you know.

Malloy: Monday mornin', Cazeneu Street, eight o'clock.

Loggo: Yeah yeah.

[**Malloy** *looks out carefully, then departs. As he gets in his car,* **Loggo** *goes to follow him but glances towards the kitchen door. We see* **Chrissie** *staring at him from the dining-room door*]

Chrissie: You soft get.

[**Loggo** *goes.* **Chrissie** *turns and opens the kitchen door. Inside the kitchen* **Angie** *is sitting on a stool. He goes to the sink, while she closes the door*]

Angie: So I'm givin' y' shite, am I?

Chrissie: Oh Jeez . . .

[**Angie** *crosses to him*]

Angie: After what you did. Look!

Chrissie: I've already looked.

Angie: Look again.

[*She holds up a bread wrapper*]

Angie: No bread. For breakfast. The kids' breakfast.

Chrissie: Oh come on, Angie. We've already talked about it —

[*He goes to the door*]

Angie: No we didn't talk about it — you threw a moody and went out there . . . [*He walks away. She follows*] to talk to the animals . . . Doctor Doolittle all right. [**Chrissie** *looks away*] There was bread last night.

Chrissie: Three slices. Angie. Three stale slices.

Angie: Yes. And you ate them.

Chrissie: No, I sandpapered the ceiling with them.

[*He goes out into the hall and leans on the banister*]

Angie: You ate them, and it was the kids' breakfast.

Chrissie: Oh don't. Just don't. How much guilt can I take, eh girl? Go on, where d' you go from bread — how about breadwinner'? Hey, hey? That's what y' really sayin', isn't it? 'Bread . . . winner'.

[*She throws the bread wrapper at him and turns her back on him*]

Chrissie: I'm going out.

[*He puts his coat on.* **Angie** *leans out into the hall from the kitchen*]

Angie: Where y' going?

Chrissie: Sell me arse on Lime Street. After all, I've tried everything else . . .

[*He goes out of the front door. She leans agains the kitchen door frame*]

9 Department of Employment; main hall

We see a high establishing shot of the body of the main hall, with claimants queueing and the counter-clerks at work.

10   Fraud section office

We see the manageress of the fraud section office, **Miss Sutcliffe***, plus her* **assistant** *in the leather jacket from 'Moonlighter'. The office has two desks, four chairs, two telephones on each desk, filing cabinets, a few charts and a large map of Greater Merseyside. Plus a semi-tropical forest of potted plants on every possible ledge and window sill. Both* **Miss Sutcliffe** *and her* **assistant** *are on the phone, but as the scene starts the* **assistant** *puts his down and begins to write.* **Miss Sutcliffe** *is writing on a note pad as she talks.*

Miss Sutcliffe: ... And your name, if I may? ... Ah yes, Minnie Mouse. Your brother Mickey often phones us up.

[*She puts the phone down and talks almost to herself, with amused contempt, as there is a knock on the door*]

Miss Sutcliffe: Along with Robert Redford, Elsie Tanner, several characters out of 'The Perishers' and Pope John Paul the Second ... Come in. [*The door opens*] We even had a Tallulah Bankhead once.

[*We see it is* **Lawton** *and* **Jackie Mills***, the driver in 'Jobs for the Boys' and the perfume representative in 'Moonlighter'*]

Miss Sutcliffe: Ah yes. Yes? You want my permission to get married?

[*They laugh,* **Lawton** *slightly too much*]

Mills: Could we see you for a few moments please, Miss Sutcliffe?

Miss Sutcliffe: Certainly. How about tomorrow?

Lawton: It's er, about our expenses, Ma'am.

Miss Sutcliffe: Oh well, make it the day after tomorrow then.

[*She smiles in dismissal, looks away, then looks back in surprise*]

Lawton: But, er, the day after tomorrow's Saturday.

Miss Sutcliffe: Yes, I know.

[**Miss Sutcliffe** *smiles blissfully.* **Lawton** *and* **Mills** *go to turn away with maiming on their mind.* **Miss Sutcliffe** *looks at her note pad*]

Miss Sutcliffe: Oh Miss Mills, here's a little something for you — a lady in Charlotte Street — perhaps you could interest her in some perfume from your catalogue?

[**Miss Sutcliffe** *again smiles at* **Mills***, who smiles back until* **Miss Sutcliffe** *looks down at her note pad, at which point* **Miss Mills'** *lip curls*]

Miss Sutcliffe: She's been accused of — erm — let me see . . . prostitution, cohabitation, mass murder, drug smuggling, and a leading role in the Afghanistan Rebellion. [*She holds out the piece of paper from her note pad*] The informant is a person by the name of Ms Minnie Mouse.

[**Mills** *takes the paper*]

Mills: Isn't that more likely to be a case for Social Security? Their Fraud Section.

Miss Sutcliffe: [*Thinks carefully*] . . . Yes.

Mills: Well, why are you giving it to me then, Miss Sutcliffe?

[**Miss Sutcliffe** *looks shocked and disapproving*]

Miss Sutcliffe: Yours not to reason why, yours but to do or die. My dear.

[**Mills** *turns away from her and approaches* **Lawton** *at the door*]

Miss Sutcliffe: Oh incidentally, Lawton, my deepest commiserations on failing your driving test. [*He looks at her and then away*] Again.

Lawton: Er, yes . . . er, thank you, Miss Sutcliffe.

[*They both go out, leaving the door open in their haste.* **Miss Sutcliffe** *smiles happily at her* **assistant** *as he goes towards the door, and glances out into the corridor before closing the door*]

Miss Sutcliffe: Yes, she has got a nice pair of legs, hasn't she . . . I don't care very much for those two. I don't know why.

Assistant: [*Flatly*] They catch people.

Miss Sutcliffe: Ah, I knew there was a reason.

[*She looks across the room at the* **assistant**, *inviting comment. She doesn't get any. There is a knock on the door, immediately followed by the door opening. We see* **Donald Moss**, **Lawton's** *associate in 'Jobs for the Boys', as he flurries into the room*]

Moss: Excuse me, sorry to bother you, apologies for the disturbance.

[**Moss** *grabs a chair, sits down, folds his arms*]

Miss Sutcliffe: Well?

Moss: No, I just thought I'd give your memory a little jog. You know — [*Points to himself*] — Donald Moss, mid-thirties, two children, house in Haydock, fraud section investigator, never a high flyer but just about where he should be in the scheme of things, comes to work every morning, sits in his office . . . and waits. And waits.

Miss Sutcliffe: You can leave. Would you like to leave? It can be arranged.

[**Miss Sutcliffe** *and her* **assistant** *exchange glances. She gets up and goes to pour herself some coffee*]

Moss: The only reason I'm here is because I don't want to be queueing out there.

Miss Sutcliffe: That's the only reason any of us are here, Donald. [*She gives him a cup of coffee, and returns to her desk*] Without them, most of us would be without a job. Correct, Derek?

Assistant: Pardon?

[**Miss Sutcliffe** *shakes her head*]

Miss Sutcliffe: [*Confidentially*] Actually, I'm saving you for a very special assignment, Donald.

Moss: ... And?

Miss Sutcliffe: We haven't got one at the moment.

Moss: You're doing this to me on purpose. You are, aren't you? Why?

[**Miss Sutcliffe** *sits*]

Miss Sutcliffe: Can I ask you something?

Moss: Only if it's worth answering.

Miss Sutcliffe: Do you like ... catching people?

[*We see the* **assistant manager** *staring dolefully*]

Moss: ... That's got nothing to do with it.

Miss Sutcliffe: Oh but it has. A lot to do with it.

Moss: No it hasn't. It's a job. I got given it, it was looked on as promotion, and I'm doing it. Or in this instance — not doing it.

Miss Sutcliffe: But you're a nice man, Donald.

[*He stands up and crosses to her desk, fast*]

Moss: Oh go and! . . . Look. The last assignment I had was two weeks ago. The builder — the feller falling out of the window — since then, nothing.

[**Miss Sutcliffe** *sighs*]

Miss Sutcliffe: . . . Come — [*She throws it in fast*] — Come up and see me sometime. No, well all right, come back later. An hour or so. And I promise I'll have found something for you to do. In the meantime . . . I think your blotting paper calls . . .

[*She turns away from him. He hesitates angrily for a second or so and then slams out of the room. The* **assistant** *looks sick*]

Miss Sutcliffe: I really like Donald when he's angry, he's ever so sweet. [*There is a pause*] You're right, you don't have to tell me. I am a cranky frustrated mature spinster employed as a kind of . . . creeping jesus sprat-catcher . . . living with an almost completely insane mother . . . and I am a woman who has recently become aware of the massive and total futility of her life.

Assistant: Ah now, come on. We agreed, didn't we — remember, we wouldn't talk about our personal problems.

Miss Sutcliffe: You mean *my* personal problems . . . It's all right. I will retire next year . . . and my mother will die soon. [*She turns away from him towards her desk*] I've made up my mind . . .

[*The phone rings on his desk. He picks it up and listens*]

Assistant: Yes . . . No, I don't need to know your name.

[*He reaches for pen and paper*]

11 Building site

Loggo *and* **Chrissie** *are walking through a building site, full of half-completed houses.* **Loggo** *is having to walk quickly to keep up with* **Chrisse**.

Chrissie: [*Angrily*] ... You're mad, you are. Mad. We're both gettin' followed, for all we know, we're both goin' t' get prosecuted f' doin' a foreigner while we're on the dole ...

Loggo: But the ...

Chrissie: And here you are, cool as a cucumber, startin' work f' Malloy of all people, and f' pound notes. What are y' trying t' do to y'self?

Loggo: I've got no money.

Chrissie: Oh well, that explains everythin'.

Loggo: An' I'm havin' a bad time with the HP — all those friggin' instalments.

Chrissie: Send the stuff back then.

Loggo: I would if I could, but I've sold most of it already ... and I'm months behind with the rent.

Chrissie: Move in with y' mam an' dad.

Loggo: I can't do that — they still think I'm a virgin — pick up a creamie an' where could I take her for a bit of recreation? Besides they're in more debt than I am.

Chrissie: Well just sod off then, Loggo. I've got my own troubles, I don't need yours.

[**Loggo** *stops astonished. He looks at* **Chrissie** *striding away.* **Chrissie** *stops*]

Chrissie: Yeah well. [*A silent apology*] I'm worried sick.

[**Loggo** *follows him and gets level*]

Loggo: Worryin' 'll do no good. Me Uncle Matthew was a

hypochondriac — never out of the X-ray unit at the Royal — barium this an' barium that — got killed by lightnin'.

Chrissie: All I want's a job, Loggo. An outside job.

Loggo: Be careful, that's what me Uncle Matthew had.

[*They are by the site agent's hut which is only a few yards away.* **Chrissie** *looks at* **Loggo**]

Chrissie: Everythin's a joke to you, isn't it?

[**Chrissie** *goes in. We focus on* **Loggo** *who quietly mimics the scene inside*]

Loggo: [*Leaning on the wall*] 'Anythin' goin' boss?' 'Sorry son, nothin'.'

[**Loggo** *clicks his fingers and points at the door. Sure enough,* **Chrissie** *comes out on cue.* **Loggo** *gets no satisfaction though*]

Loggo: Any job?

Chrissie: Oh aye, yeah, but I turned it down — didn't fancy the company car . . .

[**Chrissie** *walks off.* **Loggo** *tries to keep up with him*]

Loggo: Y' know your trouble — everythin's a joke to you . . .

12   Fraud section office

Yosser *is in the middle of a speech and clearly on his way towards breakdown. He is speeding more than ever. As he talks, the* **manageress** *is looking at her* **assistant**, *who looks at his desk. Then they both look at their watches.* **Yosser's children** *are also present:* **Dustin** *at the window,* **Jason** *by the anglepoise lamp and finally his* **daughter** *by a filing cabinet, where she is opening a drawer.*

Yosser: *And* — and on Malloy's site that particular day, the day in question, in fact, no money parted company to or from anyone. Who was there. When I was there. No money came my way. Not to my knowledge. Not when I was there. And I should know. Being there. And being me. [*He laughs, and stops dead*] Malloy on no occasion never said to me, 'Here y'are, touch for that'. [*Makes a movement with his hand indicating money being passed*]

Assistant: That's a double negative.

Yosser: Yeah well, there's two of you isn't there? And, as a matter of fact, I was there on a trial basis, but left after one wobbly wall and a short exchange of words, or words to that effect.

Miss Sutcliffe: Mr Hughes, nobody is —

Yosser: Look, here I am, a man. [*He laughs*] A man. A man. With no job. Looking for one. [*He laughs again*] It's like tryin' t' find the Scarlet Pimpernel. [*He moves in*] Have you got a job, gizza job, eh, I'd be all right, if I had a job. Honest. [*He sits*] I'd be all right. [*He shouts*] Oh yes!

[*During the following speech the **manageress** goes to the door, opens it and looks out. **Loggo** and **Chrissie** are leaning against a wall outside the door. She closes the door on them and on her way back she gently closes the filing cabinet and moves the girl away. **Yosser** seems finally to have run out of steam. She stands by the cabinet*]

Miss Sutcliffe: Well. That has been very ... long, Mr Hughes. I don't think we need to trouble you any further.

[**Yosser** *sits there*]

Miss Sutcliffe: You were, after all, only asked here to help our enquiries.

[*And* **Yosser** *sits there*]

Miss Sutcliffe: If you would like to go. Away. *Now.* Thank you.

[**Yosser** *stands. He walks towards the door and opens it. The* **children** *file out.* **Loggo** *and* **Chrissie** *are waiting still.* **Yosser** *addresses them sanely as he goes out*]

Yosser: You're all right boys, you're sound, y' can kid them soft . . . [*He laughs*]

[**Loggo** *and* **Chrissie** *move towards the door, but* **Miss Sutcliffe** *closes the door on them again. She looks at her watch and at the* **assistant** *and crosses to sit in front of him. Then she takes her shoe off*]

Miss Sutcliffe: How time flies when you're . . . Now, I know this is very naughty Derek, and after all it is your case, but I think we'll see the next two together.

Assistant: What?

Miss Sutcliffe: I know, I know, protocol and rules, memos from above, firm directives from the Ministry. But no one will know except us, and I'm not going to tell anybody.

[*She gets up and opens the door. The* **assistant** *throws down his pad in disgust*]

Miss Sutcliffe: Come in, gentlemen . . .

[**Chrissie** *and* **Loggo** *enter the fraud section office*]

13   Front of Chrissie's house

Two men are standing outside **Chrissie**'s *house at the front door. They knock. The door half opens. We see* **Angie***. She looks at the men, then at the cards they are flourishing. She slams the door fast.*

Gas man: Go an' get a chisel, Jimmy . . .

[*One man turns away and gets a tool-box from the van.*
Angie *has run round to the lounge window. When she looks
out and sees the mate return with his tool-box, she bangs the
window*]

Angie: No. Wait.

[*She returns to the hall and opens the door to let them in*]

14 Fraud section office

Miss Sutcliffe *is at her desk. Her* **assistant***, in his leather
jacket, is closing his note pad, in the centre of his desk.* **Miss
Sutcliffe** *is slightly distanced from him. He shuffles his papers
with an air of finality and puts his pen away.* **Loggo** *and*
Chrissie *are sitting at the other side of the desk, looking
suitably muted. As well as blank. They all stare at each other
for a couple of seconds. Both 'couples' exchange looks.*

Assistant: [*Formally*] I think that just about concludes
everything.

Loggo: Er yeah. Er all that y've just said, y' know, the
mumbo jumbo — what it means is er ... what does it
mean?

[*The* **assistant** *sighs with great contempt.* **Miss Sutcliffe**
intervenes, speaking pleasantly]

Miss Sutcliffe: I'm sorry, we didn't intend to confuse you.
What my colleague is saying is that it is his intention to
forward your papers for prosecution.

Loggo: Y'goin' to do us then?

Miss Sutcliffe: Well it certainly looks that way,
gentlemen.

Loggo: Ah, she called me a gentleman, now isn't that nice.
Chrissie.

Chrissie: Leave it alone, will y'.

Miss Sutcliffe: Wise advice.

Assistant: In your situation.

Miss Sutcliffe: It would be even wiser to listen to it, Mr Logmond.

Assistant: And no doubt impossible for you.

Loggo: Friggin' hell, this is a double act. Or else one's a ventriloquist.

Assistant: That's enough.

Loggo: 'Enough' — from what you've been sayin' it hasn't even started yet. I thought y' would have had y' pound of flesh when y' killed Snowy Malone.

[**Chrissie** *sighs*]

Assistant: He killed himself.

Loggo: Oh aye, yeah. He was always jumpin' from third floor windows — it was his hobby.

Assistant: None of this behaviour is helping you, you know.

Loggo: I wish I was hard. I mean I wish I had a leather jacket like that to make me hard.

Assistant: Just don't.

Loggo: Why — what are you going to do about it?

Chrissie: Forget it.

Loggo: State of it though Chrissie — had to stand on a stool t' reach manhood.

Chrissie: Y' askin' f' trouble.

Loggo: Well. We've already got it, haven't we — so screw them.

[*He turns to the* **assistant**]

Loggo: All right, go on, go 'head do what y' please — see if I care, only I'm telling you just don't walk home alone in the dark, that's all.

Assistant: I hope, for your sake, that's not a threat.

[**Loggo** *shakes his head. When he replies, he does so quietly*]

Loggo: It's a promise.

[**Miss Sutcliffe** *stands*]

Miss Sutcliffe: If I could bring the matter to a close, Mr Logmond, Mr Todd, before tempers get too heated. [*She crosses to the door*] We will keep you informed of the . . . eventualities of this particular case, but . . .

Loggo: Yeah yeah, all right. Don't bother trying to be nice, eh. It doesn't go with y' job. But at least there's one savin' grace — we won't have you minge bags followin' us around anymore, like bad smells.

Assistant: [*Eager to score any kind of point*] I wouldn't count on that, if I were you.

Loggo/Chrissie: You wha'?

[**Chrissie** *stands*]

Chrissie: What? What for?

Assistant: Because of your known and undenied activities, to possibly further the strength of our case . . . and as a deterrent. To you, and the likes of you.

Chrissie: What's your name? Hey? Come on, what's your name?

Assistant: Why?

[**Chrissie** *crosses to the* **assistant**]

Chrissie: Why? Because I'm going to report you, that's why.

Assistant: It won't do you any good.

Loggo: [*Quietly*] I know what will though . . .

Chrissie: [*Leaning over*] No one's followin' me anymore, I'm tellin' y'. No one. Havin' a job's one thing — I'm sure it must make you very proud — but usin' it to persecute people's another. 'Cos that's what y' doin'. Now what's your name?

Miss Sutcliffe: Gentlemen, gentlemen.

Loggo: There she goes again.

Chrissie: *Tell me your name.*

Loggo: Come on, we've told you ours, it's only fair. Play the white man, will y'.

Chrissie: I want your name.

Loggo: So do I. An' that's just for starters.

Loggo: Give us your friggin' name!

Assistant: . . . I don't want to, and I'm not going to. It's not . . . advisable.

[**Miss Sutcliffe** *takes over*]

Miss Sutcliffe: Absolutely correct and proper, although you can have my name if you like, you can even have my address — however, do not hesitate to register a formal complaint — gentlemen — if you feel you have not been treated in a fitting manner. But I do really suggest that our interview is now over.

[*She moves to the door, smiling warily at them*]

Assistant: For the time being.

[**Loggo** *and* **Chrissie** *hesitate.* **Chrissie** *turns to the* **assistant**]

Chrissie: I wouldn't be you. *I wouldn't be you.* Not for anythin'.

[*They move towards the door and go out. As they go* **Chrissie** *says* 'Fascist Bastards']

[*Inside the fraud section office, there is a pause before* **Miss Sutcliffe** *closes the door*]

Assistant: Scum.

Miss Sutcliffe: ... Oh I don't think so, Derek.

Assistant: I do. If they had brains they'd be dangerous.

Miss Sutcliffe: Now you may be right there. But there again, that could apply to more than those two.

[*He goes to the filing cabinet. She goes into the alcove*]

Assistant: ... Meaning?

Miss Sutcliffe: Just a general comment on mankind ... but... [*And re-enters from the alcove with a plant spray*] As I'm in charge of this deliberately feeble attempt at a fraud section, I think I should tell you straightaway that I do not intend to let the case against those two go forward.

[*She waters the plant on her desk*]

Assistant: You're what?

Miss Sutcliffe: I'm not going to let the case against those two go forward.

[*She waters the plant on the filing cabinet*]

Assistant: I've spent hours — days — this was my case.

Miss Sutcliffe: It was, yes.

[*She goes out. He slams the filing cabinet closed and follows*]

15 Corridor to main hall

She goes out into the corridor, he follows, they walk.

Miss Sutcliffe: That builder, whatsisname.

Assistant: Malloy.

Miss Sutcliffe: Malloy, I think we'll have him. Put someone on him, would you, Derek, keep me in touch, as soon as he moves we'll jump, all right? After all, he's the really naughty boy, practically making a profession out of it. I don't mind prosecuting him at all. But those two — no . . . The black boy was rather pretty though, don't you think? In a rather coarse sort of way.

Assistant: You can't mean that.

Miss Sutcliffe: About the black boy?

Assistant: No. About not prosecuting. Them.

Miss Sutcliffe: Oh but I do.

[*They reach the main hall. She turns away from him. She goes through the doorway into the area behind the grille and closes the door*]

16   Inside the counter area

They continue walking.

Assistant: But why not?

Miss Sutcliffe: Why not? Really?

Assistant: Yes.

Miss Sutcliffe: I can hear the laughter and outrage now. First of all, we manage to crash all our vehicles into a council wagon at the start of the raid, then a man is killed who is only killed, whatever we might say, because he is trying to escape from us, and finally for good measure, we are trying to arrest unemployed men who are busy building an unemployment exchange.

[*She laughs*]

[*We see* **Moss** *in his office. They reach him, and she goes in. When she speaks to* **Moss** *it is infuriatingly like a loving mother to a young child. She waters the plants in his office as she talks*]

Miss Sutcliffe: I haven't kept you waiting long, have I?

Moss: Oh no, what's three-quarters of an hour to a man who's been wasting his time for some weeks?

Miss Sutcliffe: My thoughts exactly. And ten more minutes won't make much difference, will it?

[*She walks straight past him and moves back towards the door. He gets up and goes to follow her. She closes it on him*]

Miss Sutcliffe: But don't go away, I think I might have the very thing for you.

[*He is left looking through the glass after her*]

17   Chrissie's back kitchen

We see a close up of **Angie**, *who is full of loathing. She and* **Chrissie** *are sitting on stools, facing out.*

Angie: Where were y'? *Where were y'*? Why didn't you tell me?

Chrissie: I forgot.

Angie: *You forgot*? You forgot they were coming to turn off the gas?

Chrissie: I had other things on my mind.

[**Angie** *goes to the sink, leans out, then turns*]

Angie: Yeah well . . . it doesn't matter does it? We didn't have anything to cook anyway.

[*She throws the fridge door open*]

Angie: Half a tub of marg, Monday's milk and a pound of dead lettuce.

Chrissie: That's all right, we'll save on the electricity.

[**Chrissie** *switches the fridge off at the wall plug*]

[*They move into the hall*]

Angie: Until they come to cut that off.

[*She storms past him to go up the stairs*]

18   Chrissie's stairs and landing

Chrissie *is following* **Angie** *up the stairs.*

Chrissie: Yeah. Yeah! Until they come and cut that off. And then there won't be anything left to cut off, will there, except me. But they can't cut me off though, can they — that's your department.

Angie: I can't cut off what you haven't got.

[*She goes into the toilet. Fast.* **Chrissie** *reaches the toilet door, tries to open it, but then turns away*]

Chrissie: I didn't think you could hurt me anymore.

[*He leans against the door*]

Chrissie: But there again, practice makes perfect.

[*We hear* **Angie's** *voice through the door*]

Angie: Not in your case.

[**Chrissie** *leans against the doorframe*]

Chrissie: Do you sit around all day thinking these things up? Oh that's a good one — that'll hurt him . . .

Angie: No, I sit there and wait for you to do something. You've got to do something.

[**Chrissie** *bangs on the toilet door*]

Chrissie: I *am* doing something. I'm going to court. Then I'm going to get a heavy fine. [*He is walking back and forth*] Then I'll go to jail. [*He kicks the bedroom door*] Do not stop. And you can go and live with your mother — an event you've been looking forward to for some time.

Angie: You know nothing about me, Chrissie.

Chrissie: No, y' right, y' right I don't. Of course I don't. If I'd have known you better, I would have known that. But I have this ability to live with someone for eleven years and not know anything about them. And of course, not knowing anything about you or anything come to that, I don't know what love is neither, do I.

[**Angie** *laughs from the safety of the toilet*]

Chrissie: Well it obviously isn't an empty fridge and the gas cut off.

[*The toilet flushes.* **Angie** *comes out again.* **Chrissie** *is in her way*]

Angie: Let me go past.

Chrissie: And when we get evicted, we'll be standing there in the street well and truly finished with each other. If that's what love's about.

[*He lets her go past into the bedroom where she straightens the bed*]

Chrissie: It's not my fault, you know. *Not my fault.*

Angie: Self pity, that's all I've heard from you for months. And it's pitiful.

[*He follows her and grabs her arm. He speaks with strength and anger*]

Chrissie: Look, Angie — go away, go to your mother's, go to y' sister's, go to the dogs for all I care — but go away. I'd rather have nothing than what I'm getting now. And go on your own if y' want. You don't have to take the kids and look the martyr.

[*He throws her on the bed*]

Chrissie: If you wanna go, go. And hurry up about it.

[**Chrissie** *goes into their bedroom. Closes the door behind him.* **Angie** *looks at the door*]

19   Fraud section office

Miss Sutcliffe *is sitting at her desk. She presses the intercom. The* **assistant manager** *is sitting gazing out of the window.*

Miss Sutcliffe: I'm free to take the usual heavy breathing now, Jean. [*She puts the intercom off, and glances at her watch*] Though I could do with some lunch . . . [*She looks across at her* **assistant**] You're still upset about my decision, aren't you?

[*She gets up and crosses to the alcove. The* **assistant** *is clicking his pen*]

Assistant: . . . Yes. You'll make me look a fool if this gets out.

Miss Sutcliffe: It won't 'get out', and just think of the joy you will bring into the lives of those two men when they find out.

[*He looks joylessly at her*]

Miss Sutcliffe: But I'll tell you what I'll do — just to make you happy — I'll put my little friend Donald on their tracks. Pass the time for them all.

[*She goes back in. The* **assistant** *gets up and crosses to join her*]

Assistant: But Moss was in on the arrest.

[*She is watering the plants*]

Miss Sutcliffe: Exactly.

Assistant: They know each other.

Miss Sutcliffe: Precisely.

Assistant: But for God's sake, that's illogical!

Miss Sutcliffe: So, my dear boy, is God. We're chasing people with nothing — who only want a little. Be a Christian, sport.

[*She misses a beat*]

Miss Sutcliffe: He really is a pleasant fellow, Moss, do you like Moss? I'm sure he'll find a different occupation eventually.

Assistant: But what about his safety?

[*The intercom buzzes*]

Miss Sutcliffe: Oh they wouldn't hurt him, they're nice boys.

Assistant: ... Are you ... sending me up?

[*She crosses out of the alcove*]

Miss Sutcliffe: Good heavens no, Derek. What on earth makes you think that?

[*He does not reply*]

[*She picks up the telephone, then sits down*]

Miss Sutcliffe: Of course I don't know who you are, Sir, and I wouldn't dream of asking your name, Mr - - - ah! That's a new one. Well I never! Norman Tebbit . . .

20   Chrissie's landing

Angie *walks up the stairs and stands outside their bedroom door.* **Chrissie** *is in the bedroom. They talk to each through the door.*

Angie: . . . How long're you going to stay in there?

Chrissie: Till you go away.

Angie: Ah Chrissie, you don't really want me to go away.

Chrissie: That's exactly what I want.

Angie: Right. I'm going then.

Chrissie: Good.

[*She crosses to the stairs and starts to go down*]

Angie: You can have all the benefits. [**Chrissie** *laughs*] I'll leave the family allowance book. [**Chrissie** *laughs louder*] Yeah, so it's funny, is it Chrissie? Just see how far they get you. You're always tellin' me I can't make it stretch.

[*The door opens.* **Chrissie** *is standing there*]

Chrissie: Go away!

[*The door slams in* **Angie's** *face as she runs up the stairs and crosses to the bedroom. She tries the door*]

Angie: I need a suitcase.

[*A brief pause. The door opens.* **Chrissie** *hurls a suitcase out, then closes the door*]

Angie: It isn't big enough.

[*Another pause. The door opens again. One more suitcase comes flying out. The door shuts again*]

Angie: My clothes are in the wardrobe.

[*She kneels and opens the suitcase. There is a pause, with noise. The door opens. A pile of* **Angie's** *clothing comes flying out onto the landing*]

Angie: Great, great.

[**Chrissie** *goes back in.* **Angie** *starts throwing her stuff into the suitcase.* **Chrissie** *keeps bringing more out as he finds it*]

Angie: Thank you. [*She dismisses a dress*] Don't need that.

Angie: Remember this — you made me go.

Chrissie: I won't forget it.

Angie: Don't.

Chrissie: I won't.

Angie: Good.

Chrissie: Fine.

Angie: All right.

Chrissie: Right.

Angie: Just so long as you know.

[*He slams the door*]

Angie: I'll take the kids if you want.

[*He opens the door*]

Chrissie: I don't want anything from you — especially the pressures you give me. You'd think I was the only man round here without a soddin' job. Take a look around y', girl, we form the majority around here. Only some fellers are lucky enough to have wives who recognize that fact.

Angie: All right. Right. If that's what you really believe, I'm finished.

Chrissie: I thought we were finished anyway. You don't pack your suitcase to go to the shops.

[**Angie** *slams a suitcase shut*]

Angie: What would be the point of going to the shops?

Chrissie: No y' right, y' so right, y' always are — don't go to the shops — go to friggin' hell. And don't come back!

[*He goes into the bedroom and slams the door. She goes down the stairs*]

21   Chrissie's house

As the fight continues, there is a knock on the door, **Angie** *puts the suitcases down and opens the door. Hanging onto the knocker, almost unconscious is* **George** *in his hospital escape outfit.*

Angie: Uncle . . . [*She gets hold of him, and shouts*] Chrissie! CHRISSIE!

Chrissie: I'm not in.

Angie: It's y' Uncle George, y' stupid get!

[*She can't take* **George**'s *weight anymore, and sits down on a suitcase which ludicrously collapses on her*]

Angie: Oh Christ, George.

[*As* **Chrissie** *comes running down the stairs and lifts* **George** *off, she closes the door*]

22 Fraud section office

We see **Moss**, *in close-up. He is in mid-seizure.*

Moss: But where's she gone?

Assistant: She's gone to lunch.

Moss: I've been stood outside the flaming door. How could she?

[*The* **assistant** *looks down, mumbles into his midriff*]

Assistant: She went out of the window.

Moss: Oh, go away.

Assistant: She's been out the window for some time . . .

Moss: Jeez . . . Is this her idea — to follow Logmond and Todd? [*The* **assistant** *nods*] Of course. It's so absurd, it had to be. Look, I can't follow those two.

Assistant: I know.

Moss: Well, something's got to be done.

Assistant: I know. *I know*. But you know as well as I do that this is the Civil Service, and you have to rape a Junior Minister or eat the filing cabinets before you get —

Moss: Promoted.

Assistant: Whatever.

Moss: And in the meantime I'm expected to play the tin can in a shooting gallery. [*The* **assistant** *shrugs*] Knockout.

Assistant: But if it's any consolation I've . . . and keep this to yourself . . . I've kept a file on her behaviour. [*He looks up at* **Moss**, *then looks quickly away*] It's not a thing I wanted to do, but you don't see the half. I might have to send it anonymously, but if this keeps up, I am going to send it. And I could need your support if any action is taken, Donald.

Moss: That's the last thing you'll have. [*The* **assistant**

looks up sharply at him] 'Cos I won't be here. And I've got to go now, but it's all right, don't get up, don't worry, I'll find my own way out.

[**Moss** *goes over to the window, talking as he goes, opens the window and climbs out. He turns back to face the* **assistant**]

Moss: I've got two options left open to me now — either to get pissed or follow those two. Perhaps I'll do both. Because I'll tell you frankly, and she was right, I hate this job.

[**Moss** *moves away from the window and walks off*]

23   Chrissie's living room

George *is half lying, half sitting on the sofa.* **Chrissie** *is selflessly angry. With* **George**.

Chrissie: I don't need your help — I don't want you here! What are you doin' coming here?

George: I heard. About you an' Loggo.

Chrissie: So?

[**Angie** *comes in with tea for* **George**. **Angie** *and* **Chrissie** *stand close together. Almost like a loving couple*]

George: So I know what to do — I've been through this before with the dole. I'm becomin' an expert.

[*He tries to grin.* **Angie** *stands by* **Chrissie**]

Chrissie: Yeah, on other people's behalf, but not mine, not this time, d' y' hear?

George: Aye, aye, Chrissie, no need to shout.

Chrissie: [*Calmly*] Look, Uncle George, you come first.

When y' not well, you yourself come first. I'm tellin' y' this for y' own good.

George: Oh sod that.

Angie: No, Chrissie's right.

George: If I'm treated like a sick old man I will be a sick man.

Chrissie: And if you carry on like this . . .

[*There is a knock on the front door.* **Angie** *goes to the front window*]

George: I know, it's the ambulance. People are always doin' it for me. Out of the goodness of their hearts.

Chrissie: Come on.

[**Chrissie** *goes to help* **George**, *he helps him get up*]

George: I'm OK. I'll be all right.

[**Chrissie** *goes out with him*]

Chrissie: Course y' will. And don't worry I'll sort it out. No sweat . . .

[*We see* **George** *and* **Chrissie** *leave the room.* **George** *is taken outside to the ambulance.* **Chrissie** *returns and there is silence as they stay at the window watching* **George** *get into the ambulance*]

Angie: . . . It's not just family with George, is it — he does that for everyone, doesn't he?

Chrissie: The whole estate. All creeds and denominations. And cripples and failures and head-bangers. Open house. And what does he get for it and what's his reward? He gets so sick he's never going to get better and he loses his youngest son. [*He looks up*] Thank you, Almighty God. Thank you. [*Angry*] You work in mysterious ways all right.

Angie: . . . You wouldn't have said that once.

Chrissie: Even altar boys grow up, Angie. And if you've ever believed in something, really believed in it and you find out it's not worth believing in, all you want to do is kick it till it's dead.

[*He pauses and looks at her*]

Chrissie: But you know that, don't you. That's what you feel . . . about me.

Angie: You give me no option at times.

Chrissie: Nah, I'm the one with no options. Me dad used to say to me — 'Don't get mad — get even' . . . I can't even get mad these days.

[*He goes into the hall and picks up his coat off the banister. So does she*]

Angie: You leavin' as well? We're both leaving now are we?

Chrissie: I'm going to see a man about a job and then I'm going to pick the kids up. Get some practice in for when you're not here.

[*He goes straight out without looking, leaving the door invitingly open*]

24   Front of Chrissie's house

We go outside the house. **Chrissie** *is leaning against the wall a few yards away. He looks around at the house, pensively. We go back inside to see* **Angie** *standing by the suitcases, then she picks them up, goes to the door and closes it with one of the suitcases. She begins to walk up the stairs. Outside again, we* *see* **Chrissie** *leaning against the wall. He closes his eyes and breathes out. A car comes round the corner. We hear the noise of car brakes, not harsh, but stopping quickly. Then we see* **Moss** *getting out of a Marina.* **Chrissie** *stands by the wall on the corner,* **Moss** *approaches him.* **Moss** *has the desperate air of a man no longer in control and no longer caring.*

Moss: Hi! Remember me?

Chrissie: [*Bleakly*] 'By the powers invested in me . . .'

Moss: Got it in one. Well done.

Chrissie: It was nothin'. What d' y' want?

Moss: You. I've got to follow you about. You and Logmond. No really. [*He looks around*] You don't happen to know where he is, do you? I would be fairly grateful if you two kept together. It would make my job a lot easier. [*He smiles at* **Chrissie**]

Chrissie: If this is a joke, I can supply the punch-line.

[**Chrissie**, *then* **Moss**, *start walking*]

Moss: No it's no joke, it's an outright madness. Now let me see, there's two of you, and only one of me, so if you insist on not being together, I'll have to follow you in turns. Who do you think should go first? Do you want to toss for it?

[*He searches in his pocket for a penny*]

Moss: Oh and by the way, I won't be working nights or weekends.

[*They stop*]

Chrissie: What's all this about?

Moss: You know on Christmas Day in the First World War, when the enemy troops from both sides got together in No Man's Land and made friends and played football.

[**Chrissie** *stares at him*]

Moss: And just for once forgot the absolute lunacy of what they were doing to each other?

Chrissie: . . . Yeah.

Moss: Well. This is it, pal. This is Christmas Day.

[*He smiles at* **Chrissie**]

Moss: Oh. And don't worry, because I know something you don't know. You see, before long we're both going back behind the lines.

[*He winks at* **Chrissie** *and goes back to the car. When he reaches it he turns to face* **Chrissie**. **Chrissie** *looks confused*]

Moss: Happy New Year. Pal.

[*He gets in the car.* **Chrissie** *begins to walk away*]

25   Moss's car

Moss *is sitting in the car alone and only then do we see the abject hopelessness of the man. He looks around, his arms on his lap. He reaches for his CB microphone.*

Moss: No! No, no, no. Not me. This is Donald Moss. [*He searches for things in his pocket*] Here's my warrant card. [*He throws it down*] Me little tin badge. [*He throws it down*] Here's my office keys and here's my plastic government issue briefcase . . . signing off. [*He gets out of the car*] Oh, and here's the keys to the car. It's low on oil. [*He walks towards the pavement*] I'd sooner be back on the counter. In Wigan. [*He throws the keys down the drain*]

26   Chrissie's living room

Chrissie, Angie *and their two children,* **Justine** *and* **Clare,** *aged ten and eight, all well wrapped up, are watching the end of the children's programmes on BBC1, just before the early-evening News. A small two-bar electric fire is in front of the gas fire. There is a ring at the door.* **Angie** *is nearest to the door and goes out.* **Chrissie** *follows to the lounge doorway.* **Angie** *opens the front door to* **Loggo** *and* **Malloy.** *Angrily, she comes back to the lounge, she doesn't look at* **Chrissie.**

Angie: It's for you.

[**Chrissie** *crosses into the hall*]

27   Chrissie's hall

He goes into the hallway, closing the sitting-room door. **Malloy** *and* **Loggo** *are outside, anxious. There is a pause as* **Chrissie** *looks at them.*

Chrissie: Y' got the message then?

[**Malloy** *nods*]

Chrissie: . . . Yeah well, you'd better come in . . .

28   Chrissie's hall

As **Malloy** *and* **Loggo** *are about to step inside the house, we see and hear a van pulling to a halt outside the house. It is driven by the* **assistant manager.** **Lawton,** *who is the passenger, bounces out eagerly and runs towards* **Chrissie's** *open door. The* **assistant manager** *gets out of the van as well.* **Chrissie** *tries to slam the door on* **Loggo** *and* **Malloy.**

Chrissie: Oh shit.

[**Loggo** *and* **Malloy** *push in past him fast*]

29   Chrissie's hall/passage to the back kitchen

Malloy *tries to blunder into* **Chrissie's** *living room but is dragged back by* **Loggo**, *who pushes him into the kitchen. They wrestle and* **Loggo** *runs through the kitchen.* **Angie** *has come out into the hall.*

Angie: What the hell . . .

[*At the front door,* **Chrissie** *tries to stop* **Lawton** *as he pushes at the front door and keeps it open*]

Lawton: Avon calling.

[**Loggo** *and* **Malloy** *run out the back.* **Lawton** *and the* **assistant manager** *follow, pushing arrogantly past* **Chrissie**. *They also push* **Angie** *aside*]

Assistant: Excuse me love.

[**Chrissie** *shouts*]

30   Chrissie's back yard

Loggo *crashes into the back yard, followed by* **Malloy**. *They stop while* **Loggo** *opens* **Chrissie's** *back yard door. Waiting behind it are two heavy gentlemen.* **Loggo** *looks for escape desperately. He jumps over the goose pen and the side wall and out.* **Malloy**, *also trying to escape, turns back towards* **Lawton** *and the* **assistant manager**, *who come out of the house and take hold of* **Malloy** *only.* **Loggo** *meets the second 'heavy' in the alley then turns and sees* **Lawton**, *the* **assistant manager** *and* **Malloy** *and the other two men.* **Loggo** *looks at them, then backs off, flinching slightly as they walk past, half expecting a clout. He runs off totally puzzled.* **Lawton** *and the* **assistant manager** *take* **Malloy** *along the alley.*

Malloy: [*Pathetically*] But why me? What about them?

Assistant: You're not pretty.

Malloy: What?

Assistant: Forget it.

[*They lead him away.* **Chrissie** *has moved a pace or two
into the alley. He turns and walks back to the kitchen door.*
Angie *slams it on him. He turns away*]

31   Miss Sutcliffe's flat

We see **Miss Sutcliffe** *is at her dining table. The food she
organized earlier in the day is on the table. So is the bottle of
wine. She is on the phone. As the phone call continues we
become aware that it is from her* **assistant***.*

Miss Sutcliffe: ... yes I know, I know, it's fascinating,
Derek, the three of them together. Indeed, in the same
house at the same time. Perhaps they're friends, no? ...

[*As her* **assistant** *talks,* **Miss Sutcliffe** *hears her* **mother's**
*bedroom door open. She looks across. We see a salad dinner
on a tray. A hand edges out from the bedroom and takes the
tray slowly off the floor. The door closes.* **Miss Sutcliffe**
smiles bitterly]

Miss Sutcliffe: Yes Derek, no Derek, a coincidence,
Derek, a mere accident of fate, time and event. And not to
be pursued ... just Malloy, that's my boy. [*She giggles*] ...
Thank you anyway, Derek, but you will have to excuse me, I
do have to go now. You see I'm very bored.

[*She puts the phone down, sits there, all malice and warmth,
and begins to eat. She hears a window being opened in her*
mother's *bedroom.* **Miss Sutcliffe** *stops eating and
listens. There is a distant crash of crockery, seeming to be
from outside. She looks to the dining room window, then to
her* **mother's** *door. She approaches, opens the door gently*]

and looks in. We see her **mother's** *bedroom, one of the windows open wide, the curtains blowing and no sign of her* **mother.** **Miss Sutcliffe** *goes to the window quickly and looks out. Down below, on the ground, we see the remnants of the salad, the smashed plates, the teapot, the milk jug, and the cup. But no* **mother.** **Miss Sutcliffe** *looks around the room, focuses finally on a big old-fashioned wardrobe and approaches it. When she flings open both doors we see her* **mother** *in a nightgown, sitting in the bottom corner of the wardrobe with a quietly insane and victorious smile.* **Miss Sutcliffe** *slams both the doors shut, stares at the wardrobe for a second or two then turns the key to the doors of the wardrobe and locks them. She walks away*]

32 Chrissie's back kitchen/dining room

Angie *is collecting plates. She goes into the kitchen.* **Chrissie** *is there when she enters with three plates, knives and forks.*

Chrissie: Still not speakin' to me?

[*No answer, except she scrapes plates*]

Chrissie: Well, at least that's one question answered.

[**Angie** *moves back to collect the bread and sauce bottles, and goes back into the kitchen to put them away*]

Chrissie: I thought you might have some comment to make about what happened before with Malloy. Even if it was just to express your disgust and contempt as . . .

Angie: I'd rather be starving.

[*She goes back into the dining room*]

Chrissie: Oh great. Just like a woman. This afternoon it was my fault we were starving. [*He follows*] But tonight you'd rather starve. Not that you have, though. [*He goes* *back into the kitchen*] Does it amuse you not to make my tea? And then sit and sulk for three hours?

[*She turns away*]

Chrissie: The best bit though was putting the kids to bed. Without sending them in to me. Leprosy as well, hey?

Angie: I hate you. [**Angie** *goes into the lounge*]

Chrissie: Of course you do. But it's all right. I don't mind, because you don't know anything about anything. You — you think that life's like the inside of a Wendy House. And I'm only there to look after the dolls.

[*He follows her into the dining room, then into the lounge. She flies at him, fingernails to the front.* **Chrissie** *parries her attempts to scratch and hit him. He takes hold of her hands and is too strong for her. But he looks at her rage and her eyes*]

Chrissie: Oh yeah. You as well, eh . . . Go on then. Why not, one free shot.

[*He lets go of her and stands there.* **Angie** *begins to batter him, she hits him in the face, on the chest and arms and shoulders, screaming. He falls back. She goes on battering him. He puts his hands over his head in surrender*]

Angie: For once in your life, stand up for yourself. Fight back. Fight back . . .

[*She cannot carry on. She leans on arm of chair. Their* **younger daughter** *has appeared on the stairs. She is watching*]

Chrissie: It's all right, Justine. Me and mummy are just playing at wrestling. And mummy's winning.

[**Angie** *still leans on the chair.* **Chrissie** *walks to the stairs, picks up* **Justine**]

Chrissie: Hey come on, come on ... we're only playing. Ssshh.

[*He takes* **Justine** *upstairs*]

33 Chrissie's living room

Angie *is in a chair, with her back turned to the door. She is smoking a cigarette.* **Chrissie** *enters and closes the door.*

Chrissie: She's asleep. And that's my last cigarette.

[**Angie** *throws it at him. It hits him but he ignores it, leaves it on the carpet. He sits down. They both look at the cigarette which is smouldering*]

Chrissie: It's all right — I've stopped smoking.

Angie: So have I.

Chrissie: That's what I call a sudden decision.

[*There is a pause*]

Chrissie: I'm not picking it up.

Angie: Neither am I.

Chrissie: You threw it.

Angie: You never caught it.

Chrissie: My dad's bigger than your dad.

Angie: I've got a big brother.

Chrissie: But I can fight him. Anyway, he's in Australia. [**Chrissie** *smiles*]

Angie: I'm not making friends.

[**Chrissie** *puts his finger to his lips and makes blubbering baby noises. She turns away from him*]

Angie: You're not funny.

Chrissie: I'm not laughing.

[**Angie** *bends down and picks up the cigarette*]

Chrissie: I thought you'd stopped.

Angie: Yeah well. I've started again.

Chrissie: No will-power, have you?

Angie: Oh! Sod off, Chrissie. I used to think you were funny, but not any more.

Chrissie: Isn't it strange — I feel exactly the opposite about you. You're becoming more hysterical by the minute.

[*There is a long pause as* **Angie** *finishes the cigarette. Then she stubs it out*]

Chrissie: Just like the home life of our gracious queen.

Angie: *Shut up!* I'm going to bed.

[*She stands up, strides off up stairs*]

Chrissie: Is that an invitation?

[**Angie** *ignores him and goes out. He stops being funny immediately*]

Chrissie: Obviously not . . .

[**Chrissie** *stands and goes over to where she was sitting. He inspects the cigarette end, and dismisses, reluctantly, the chances of smoking it. He walks back towards the couch, reaches out with his foot and boots the couch hard against the wall. As it hits the wall, the couch makes a jangling noise. He throws the cushions off.* **Chrissie** *looks at the couch in a new light. He tilts it onto its back. He hears the jangle of money again, and he rips the fabric off the seam at the bottom end. He puts his hand into the insides of the couch, feels around and brings out a crumpled packet of cigarettes.*

When he opens it and sees it is nearly full, he chuckles fit to bust. He puts them on top of the sofa, then takes out half an ancient hamburger, some spilt chips, several crayons, a few coppers and two 50p pieces. He tries to put them on the sofa, fails and so puts them on the table. He rips the rest of the bottom of the sofa off, finds a Liverpool FC programme, and then to his sublime joy, a five-pound note. Almost infantile, certainly childish in his pleasure, he holds it up to the light, inspects it and kisses it]

34 Bedroom

Night time. **Angie** *is in bed, tossing and turning. She hears* **Chrissie** *singing 'Memories are made of this'.*

35 Chrissie's living room

Chrissie *is lying on the sofa with a half-bottle of whisky and four cans of lager, plus a huge portion of chips. He is just completing a demolition job on the chips. He lifts the couch up and puts the chip paper down the side of the sofa. He sings quietly 'Memories are made of this'.*

36 Bedroom

Angie *is in bed as before. She hears* **Chrissie** *still singing.*

37 Chrissie's living room

We see the clock on the mantlepiece. It is quarter to seven and still dark outside. We come back to **Chrissie***, who is asleep against the couch, but just waking up. Around him are the lager cans and the empty whisky bottle. He groans and sucks in his* *breath. He looks at the evidence of his drinking, contemplates the base of the couch, but thinks better of it. He gets to his feet, picking up the lager cans and whisky bottle. As he walks into the hall, he drops a can on the floor.*

38 Kid's bedroom

The kids are in bed together. One of them wakes up.

39 Hall

Chrissie *bends down to pick up the can, and drops another. Then he drops the lot.*

Chrissie: Frig it. Frig it.

[*He walks to the bottom of the stairs*]

40 Chrissie's bedroom

Angie *has her back turned as* **Chrissie** *enters and starts to get undressed. The argument starts immediately. Throughout the scene he undresses, gets into bed, and as soon as he is in bed, the argument is such that he gets right out again and puts on his clothes.*

Chrissie: Angie . . .

Angie: *What*? It's nearly seven o'clock, d' you know that?

Chrissie: Yeah, but . . .

Angie: You went out last night.

Chrissie: I know . . .

Angie: If you went for a drink I'll never talk to you again.

Chrissie: Promises, promises . . . No . . . I want to talk.

Angie: You are doing.

Chrissie: No . . .

Angie: I haven't slept.

Chrissie: I came up last night and you were fast.

Angie: I was pretending. I heard you, but I was pretending.

Chrissie: So was I. I never came up.

[*She turns away from him, covering the blankets around herself*]

Chrissie: Angie. Angie. *Angie.*

[*She covers her head up now*]

Chrissie: Angie. This is . . . our life . . . and I wish I was dead. But this is how it is at the moment. This is the way of our life . . . [*He laughs, throwing the next sentence away*] It's a way of life. The only trouble is, it's no way to live. I know that . . . look, you don't have to go all miserable and bastard like and fight with me. [*He gets into bed*]

Angie: [*From beneath the bedclothes*] You have been drinking.

[**Chrissie** *closes his eyes*]

Chrissie: I had a job, Angie. It wasn't a bad job, and I was good at it. I laid the roads, girl. *I laid the roads.* Motorways, lay-bys, country lanes.

Angie: Chrissie . . .

Chrissie: No, no. Let me finish. I could tamper and grit like nobody you ever saw. Nobody put the black stuff down quite like me. [*He shrugs*] But I lost that job, it was all right, I deserved to lose it, I was a dickhead — but haven't we all been at one time or another — haven't we all woken up the next mornin' an' gone 'oh Jesus, did I do that'? Yeah, well, once you could get away with it. But not now. That's the problem.

[*He lies back.* **Angie** *turns back to him, sits up in bed*]

Angie: I am twenty-eight years old, Chrissie . . .

Chrissie: What's that got to do with?

Angie: No, look. Let me finish, all right. I am twenty-eight, I married you when I was seventeen. I was a mother at eighteen. Now I'm not blaming you for that, I'm not.

[*He lies under the covers*]

Angie: It takes two to tango. But I'm a person you kn—

[*The alarm clock goes off at the side of the bed. She thumps it into silence*]

Angie: — I live and breathe, and fart after five lager and limes. I have a mind up here. And it's screaming Chrissie. I mean it can't — it can't take much more. I mean, it was never much fun early on, how could it be . . . babies and sick and nappies and no sleep at nights — it's not like you imagine it to be, it's not like it is in the *Woman's Own*. But I loved you. I love the kids.

Chrissie: I like the past tense with me.

Angie: No no no. See, you never listen to me.

[*There is a pause. He sighs*]

Angie: What I'm . . . the thing is . . . aaaaaaaahhhhhhhh! . . . I've never had a life outside of you and Justine and Clare. That's all. But I was going to. I was going to do a lot. Back to college. Job of my own. Out in the world. 'Hi Angie' . . . this was going to be my time. And what's happened instead — we're not, we're not even livin' hand to mouth.

Chrissie: All down to me, eh? Good old Chrissie, done it again.

Angie:　No!

Chrissie:　Absolute crap, Angie. [*He gets out of bed and gets dressed fast and erratically*] Don't look at me if you're not going to college, don't look at me if you've got no life, don't.

[**Angie** *gets up in the bed*]

Angie:　Oh you, you, you. You never listen to me!

Chrissie:　What is there to listen to?

Angie:　So that's what you think — that's how much you know. And I'm the one who's supposed to know nothing! Well, not stood against you, I'm not.

Chrissie:　Oh behave yourself — you're not even making sense.

Angie:　What sense is there to make, Chrissie? What is it? What is there? What did I dream of — and where is it? [*She points towards the children's bedroom*] What are they going to be doing in ten years' time? Are they still going to be wearing hand-me-downs at eighteen and twenty? What are we bringing them up for — and what is the point of livin' our lives when . . . when y'get up in the mornin' and it's all downhill from then on . . . two ounces of spam and a quarter of brawn and any stale . . . look!

[*She grabs a shoe from the side of the bed, turns it so that the sole faces* **Chrissie**, *then realizes that it's the wrong one. She hurls it away, and gets the other one.* **Chrissie** *laughs. She shows him the shoe. There is a hole in the shoe, temporarily filled with cardboard*]

Angie:　Look —

Chrissie:　Yeah, well. Walk on one leg, you'll be all right.

[**Angie** *pushes him on to the floor*]

Angie:　It's not funny, It's not friggin' funny. I've had enough of that — if you don't laugh, you'll cry — I've heard it for years — this stupid soddin' city's full of it — well, why don't you cry — why don't you scream — why don't you fight back, you bastard. Fight back. They're knockin' the shite an' stuffin' out of you, Chrissie Todd, and if you haven't had enough, I have.

Chrissie: . . . And what do you think it's like for me? Hey? A second-class citizen. A second-rate man. With no money and no job . . . and no . . . no place!

[**Angie** *turns away from him. She speaks flatly*]

Angie: Tell it to the kids, Chrissie, tell it to the cupboards and the fridge. See how full y' words can make them. And when you've done that, make breakfast — and if y' do, y'll have found a job — because y'll be a soddin' magician.

[**Chrissie** *goes towards the door*]

Chrissie: Yeah, I'll fill them, you see if I don't. I'll fill them — and I hope you enjoy it.

[*He crashes out of the room and down the stairs. We hear him banging into the back kitchen. We stay with* **Angie** *as she slumps on to the bed. We hear the kitchen door leading to the yard as it opens. We hear* **Chrissie** *crashing about. We see the* **children** *wake up. We see* **Angie** *looking up, then sitting up on the bed*]

41   Chrissie's back yard

The **children** *come to the window and look down as they hear* **Chrissie** *coming out of the house and kicking a bucket.* **Chrissie** *throws the chickens out of their pen into the yard. The* **children** *look out.* **Chrissie** *has difficulty in getting all the* *chickens out. We see* **Angie** *join the* **children** *at the window, then pull them away.*

42   Landing; Chrissie's house

Angie *pushes the* **children** *from their bedroom into the main bedroom. They are both scared and shouting.*

Children: What is he doing . . . is he hurting them . . . what is he doing?

Angie: He's not doing anything . . . get in there and stay . . .

Children: What's he doing?

Angie: Get in . . . get in. Just get in. All right?

[*She closes the door on them and puts on her dressing-gown as she races down the stairs*]

43   Chrissie's back yard; dawn

The geese and the ferret are agitated. We see **Angie** *arrive at the back door in her dressing-gown, looking into the yard as* **Chrissie** *approaches. He has a cardboard box in his arms.* **Chrissie** *empties the box so that the chickens and pigeons drop limply around her feet.*

Chrissie: Here y' are, chicken for a week, and as much pigeon pie as y' can eat.

[**Chrissie** *throws the box away, turns from* **Angie** *and lifts the gun. He loads it*]

Chrissie: And goose for Sunday.

[*We see the geese.* **Angie** *moves to* **Chrissie'***s side, grabs* *hold of his arm. She keeps away from his range of fire as she tries to stop him*]

Angie: Chrissie, don't. Jesus, don't.

[*He pushes her away to the back door and aims at the geese. We see them in their pen. Then we focus on* **Chrissie** *as he is about to pull the trigger. He fires both barrels. Feathers fly whilst the rabbits tremble. One of them has a substantial splattering of blood across its white fur.* **Chrissie** *looks around him. He cries out and hurls the gun away from himself. He sits on the tea chest, and cries and cries and cries. Slowly* **Angie** *moves towards him as he sits with his head in his hands, openly weeping. She goes down on her haunches, facing him, then puts her hands on his knees. She too is upset, and near to tears. He finally looks down at her hands, sees the blood and wipes it away. He tries to control himself and takes hold of her hands. He looks down at her, then looks slightly to her side, at the rabbit. He looks back. Eventually he speaks*]

Chrissie: Somebody'd better wash the blood off that rabbit . . .

[**Angie** *half laughs, half cries at the ridiculousness of his words. After a time he joins her in laughter and tears. The action freezes*]

Graeme Souness as himself in Yosser's Story`

Yosser's Story

First shown on BBC2 on 31 October 1982

Characters

Yosser Hughes
Maureen Hughes, his wife
Jason Hughes
Anne Marie Hughes } their children
Dustin Hughes
Chrissie Todd
Loggo Logmond
George Malone
Wino
Doctor
Priest
DoE clerk
Moey
School attendance officer
Health visitor
Malloy, a building contractor
Pub manager
Electrician
Rent man
Morgan, a social worker
Veronica, another social worker
Eviction man
Scarface policeman

Boy with air gun
Hospital patient
Nosebleed policeman
Police driver
Graeme Souness } the Liverpool FC players
Sammy Lee

Yosser's Story

---

1   Yosser's dream

Yosser *and his three* **children** *are exploring the inside of a Folly. We see the outside of the Folly. They look out and see the following events.*

2   Yosser's dream: a lake

The scene is a lake at evening time, in a Liverpool park. There are shadows on the ground and the sun is coming through the trees. Boats are being rowed on the lake. We see **Yosser** *approaching the water's edge with his* **children.** *All four are fully clothed. A number of people sitting on the bank watch them as they march on towards the lake. They step right in and walk till they have to swim. The eldest boy and girl can swim well. The youngest has to hold on to* **Yosser** *as it gets deeper.* **Yosser** *treads water, then turns to the water's edge where the people have gathered. He whispers.*

Yosser: I'm Yosser Hughes.

[*His face remains expressionless. The two eldest are swimming. The youngest has disappeared.* **Yosser** *looks around*]

Yosser: Dustin. Dustin. Dustin!

[*As he turns, a boat goes slowly past him and the* **children**. *The boat is being rowed by a man with his back turned to us. But we see he is dressed in a surgeon's tunic and mask. Lying in the boat, in his pyjamas with a pillow behind his head, is* **George**. *He looks at* **Yosser** *as he goes past*]

Yosser: George, George, it's Yosser. Where's Dustin? George, where's Dustin? Dustin!

[**George** *shakes his head. As* **Yosser** *watches the boat going away, his eldest boy takes hold of him.* **Yosser** *looks away from* **George**, *bewildered and hurt. He puts his arms around his two clinging* **children** *and takes them under the water for the first time. We see the empty lake.* **Yosser** *and* **Jason**, *the eldest, re-emerge.* **Yosser** *looks around and cries out*]

Yosser: Anne Marie, Anne Marie! Dustin!

[*Another boat is approaching. We see* **Loggo** *and* **Chrissie**. *They are dressed like contestants at the Henley Regatta.* **Chrissie** *is the cox and* **Loggo** *is on the oars. They sweep past him, glance once at him in almost mechanical unison and then dismiss him*]

Yosser: Boys, boys, boys, it's me, Yosser. I'm losing my children, boys, boys.

[*No reply. The crowds around the edge of the lake wave and* **Yosser** *takes* **Jason** *down for a second time. We see them underwater. There is silence. A boat rows by. He surfaces alone.* **Yosser** *looks all round him. We see, from his point of view,* **Maureen**, *his wife, in another rowing boat, approaching him. A man who will later be identified as* **Moey** *is rowing the boat.* **Maureen** *is dressed to overkill. The boat gets closer to* **Yosser** *than all the others, and just misses him, but* **Maureen** *doesn't even look at him.* **Yosser** *shouts to her as the boat is parallel with him*]

Yosser: Maureen, Maureen . . . Maureen! It's me, Maureen. I've lost them, Maureen, it's me!

[*The waves from the boat splash over him as it goes away. And* **Yosser** *closes his eyes. He pushes up in the water and then hurtles down. We see him alone underwater. Into blackness*]

3 Yosser's bedroom

Blackness. Then in the darkness, we hear **Yosser** *mumbling, then shouting.*

Yosser: No . . . no . . . No! Oh no.

[*He is breathing heavily. A light goes on. We are in* **Yosser's** *bedroom. His hand still on the dangling flex for the light switch, he looks over and sees his* **children** *all fast asleep in the double bed. He sits up in bed still breathing hard*]

4 Department of Employment; main hall

The **counter-clerk** *is behind a grille.* **Yosser** *is leaning forward, staring straight ahead through the wire. He is framed by his* **children***. They all look desperately tired and uncared for.* **Yosser** *appears to be in a mood of manic calm as he stares at the* **clerk***.*

Clerk: . . . Mr Hughes. Mr Hughes . . . I can't help you if you don't tell me what you want. I have your details here, but if you won't speak to me . . . is it . . . is it your children, their mother . . . it's not my job to . . . but you don't seem to be drawing your full entitled . . . benefits . . . would you like to talk to anyone else about your . . . position? Mr Hughes? Mr Hughes? . . . Mr Hughes. [*Quietly*] Mr Hughes, my wife is a social worker, I can ask her to call in and see . . .

[**Yosser** *nods his head once and mumbles*]

Clerk: What? Pardon, Mr Hughes. Did you say something then?

[**Yosser** *leans forward, with apparent menace. But then he speaks*]

Yosser: Goodbye.

5   Malloy's plant shed

We see **Malloy**, *the builder established in the previous plays. He is in his plant shed, fussing over and setting up a 30-cwt power hammer. We hear* **Yosser** *from the doorway.*

Yosser: Gizza job, go —

[**Malloy** *turns and sees* **Yosser** *and the* **children** *in the doorway*]

Yosser: Oh. Right. Fair enough. [*He turns away, then turns back*] Go on though, I can do that, I know how to work them.

[**Malloy** *doesn't look at* **Yosser**. *He speaks flatly*]

Malloy: I haven't got any jobs. There are no jobs here anymore. For one reason or another. I laid off fourteen men yesterday. I grew up with some of them.

[**Malloy** *tests the power hammer. It comes crashing down violently*]

Malloy: Good fun hey?

Yosser: Gizza job.

[*But* **Yosser** *is already walking away with his* **children**. **Malloy** *watches him go, then walks towards the door and locks it. He walks back and kneels down, almost sideways,*

*beneath the power hammer so that his head is directly
beneath the hammer.* **Malloy** *lies still. Then he reaches
around the side towards the button to operate the
hammer*]

6 Outside plant shed

We see **Yosser** *and his* **children** *walking away from the plant
shed. We hear the echoing bang from the power hammer.*
Yosser's children *look around.* **Yosser** *keeps going. He
speaks flatly.*

Yosser: I could have done that . . .

7 Playing field

Yosser *is on a school playing field with his* **children**. *He is
following a solitary man who is marking the touchline for a
football pitch. The man has already heard enough.*

Yosser: Gizza job, go on, gizzit . . . gizza go, go on. I
could do that. You only have to walk straight. I can walk
straight, go on, gizza job, go on, gizza go.

[*The man does a right-angle turn at the corner of the pitch,
and heads towards the goalposts. He has gone faster and
faster to try and get away. He doesn't look back.* **Yosser**
doesn't make the turn with him but keeps walking straight]

Yosser: . . . I can put the nets up as well . . .

[*His* **children** *run to join him*]

8 Playground

It is daytime. We are in a Liverpool park. There is a play area with swings, a slide, monkey ladders, and a merry-go-round. Underneath a tree sit **Yosser** *and his* **children**, *watching.* **Dustin** *is playing with a stick. He seems happy.*

Dustin: What are we going to do?

Anne Marie: Dunno.

> [*She leans on* **Yosser**. *We see what they are watching: a family, a father and mother and three children in the play area. They are enjoying themselves. The mother and father are pushing the children on the swings.* **Yosser** *and his* **children** *watch. Then the mother gets on the slide and the father catches her and picks her up. They are laughing happily, while* **Yosser** *and the* **children** *continue to watch. As a solitary magpie takes off from the ground, we see* **Yosser** *turn sharply away from the scene and butt the tree as hard as he can. Four times. The* **children** *keep facing out, and the magpie flies off*]

9   Flat (living room)

Maureen *is peeping out and down through closed curtains of a high-rise flat.* **Moey**, *the man she is living with, is in the hall tuning his drums. She crosses, sits on the sofa and calls 'Moey' then gets up and looks out of the window.*

Maureen: Moey. Do something, Moey!

Moey: Yeah all right. [*He does nothing and carries on tuning*]

Maureen: . . . Well, what're you going to do then?

> [**Moey** *comes to the door*]

Moey: Have a heart attack.

> [*We see* **Moey** *front on. He has been beaten black and blue*]

Moey: Listen Maureen, it's been very nice and all that, but I'm not a brave man and I don't want to live with you anymore. Or to be more specific. I don't want you to live with me anymore.

[**Maureen** *gets up and rushes to* **Moey***. He grabs her*]

Moey: Maureen I want you to go. Now.

[*She breaks away.* **Moey** *goes back into the hall, where she joins him. When he starts playing the bongos, she then crosses into the bedroom muttering*]

Moey: Bastard, Bastard.

[**Moey** *cleans the bongos*]

Maureen: But what about him?

Moey: [*Flatly*] Go out the back way. Dig a tunnel. Get airlifted out, wait till it goes dark. But go. [*He crosses into the bedroom to collect his costume then goes out again*]

Maureen: But where am I going to go?

[*There is a long pause*]

Moey: South America?

[*She gestures two fingers at* **Moey** *and the world in general*]

10   The back of the flats

Maureen, *struggling with the weight of two suitcases, slips out of the block of high-rise flats. As she approaches a recess near a lamp-post, out of the shadows of the recess and into the light comes* **Yosser**, *in a surge of movement.*

Maureen: For Christ's sake leave me alone you bastard, I don't want you anymore.

[*She squeals and tries to knee him. He pushes her against the lamp-post as she drops her suitcases on the ground.* **Yosser** *takes hold of* **Maureen** *by the hair and leans back as if to butt her, but as he brings his head forward with force, he moves her head sideways and deliberately butts the lamp-post. It obviously hurts. He moves her head back into place in front of the lamp-post. We see* **Yosser's children** *peering out of the recess*]

Yosser: Come home. Please.

[*He lets go of her hair and smiles. She laughs out loud. But it is half-laugh, half-sob. He looks at her for a second or so, and as she stands there, he walks off, followed as always by his* **children**, *in and out of the pools of light thrown by the street-lamps. We just hear his* **two younger children** *speak, totally without pathos, as they walk at either side of* **Yosser**, *each holding his hand*]

Anne Marie: She used to be our mummy.

Dustin: I know.

[*In the distance* **Maureen** *starts to collect up her things*]

11   Yosser's house

There is a **man** *knocking at* **Yosser's** *door. He turns to see* **Yosser** *and his three* **children** *approaching.* **Yosser**, *carrying a Tesco bag, and apparently in a hurry ignores him, opens the door and goes inside with the* **children**. *As this happens, the* **man** *speaks.*

School attendance officer: Mr Hughes? Mr Hughes, my name's Watkins, I'm the schools' attendance officer for the area. The headmistress informs me that your children have not been attending of late —

[The door closes]

School attendance officer: Mr Hughes ...

[Knocks on the door again. But there is no reply. **Mr Watkins** *puts an official-looking envelope through the letterbox. As he turns away, the envelope comes flying out again but he does not see it and carries on walking away]*

12   Yosser's kitchen and back kitchen

The kitchen is in a fine mess, with black bin bags overflowing and left by the back door, plates piled high in the sink, and everything in, on, or around the cooker blackened and burnt. A patch on the wall above the cooker looks as though it has caught fire. In one corner, several kittens and a cat are playing. **Yosser** *is at the cooker murdering a pan of fish fingers. Burning toast sends smoke signals from the grill.* **Yosser** *is doing — and saying — everything at a frenetic pace. The* **three children** *are waiting at the table in the back kitchen. The eldest is laying the table. The other two are playing with the kittens.*

Yosser: You wanna dinner — you can have a dinner. I can cook, course I can cook, sod the chippy, leave it to me.

[He throws the black and dead toast out from under the grill. It lands somewhere near a black bin bag. He starts again]

Yosser: Never let it be said, even though they might say it. I can manage, no sweat, I can cook, course I can cook, who says I can't.

[He turns the flame under the fish fingers even higher then swings round towards his **children***]*

Yosser: Won't be long now.

[*The* **children** *wait patiently while we hear sounds of disaster coming from the kitchen*]

13   Chip shop

We cut to **Yosser** *coming glumly out of a chip shop with a large bag of chips in his hands. The* **children** *are in attendance. He starts to walk away. The* **children** *run after him.*

14   Front door of Yosser's house

The door-knocker is rapped loudly. Inside the hall it is dark, but we see **Yosser's** *eldest boy,* **Jason,** *walk to the front door in his pyjamas. He opens the door. We see a* **health visitor** *facing him. She is a lady of brisk, pleasant, matronly authority.*

Health visitor: Now you'll be Jason, won't you? There's a good boy, I've just come to have a few words with your father.

15   Hall/living room

The **health visitor** *walks straight past the boy and into the small hallway. Meanwhile, at the top of the stairs, the* **two youngest children** *are peeping around the corner of the banisters but they dart back as she looks. She walks into the living room and has a good look round.* **Jason** *follows her to the door.*

Health visitor: Is your Dad still in bed?

[**Jason** *nods, and she says the next line to herself as she writes in her file*]

Health visitor: Oh well, it is only ten to twelve. [*She closes her file*] You don't mind if I wash my hands do you, dear?

[*As she marches off to the kitchen without waiting for a reply — or expecting one — the child has no option. We hear him hurry out of the living room and up the stairs*]

16   Back kitchen

She enters the back kitchen, and as she does so we follow her and see her view of the debris. Despite the state of it she does not flicker, but simply writes some more in her file. Even after opening a cupboard she does not wash her hands. Finally she turns around as we see **Yosser** *in a shirt and underpants arrive at the kitchen door. His* **children** *again, are behind him.* **Yosser** *whispers.*

Yosser: I know what you've come for. Wash your hands, my arse.

17   Back kitchen

Yosser *is on his hands and knees in the back kitchen, scrubbing furiously at the floor. The bin bags have gone and the sink is empty. The cooker and work surfaces look a great deal cleaner. He appears to be talking to himself.*

Yosser: Well all right. So that's the game, yeah well, yeah yeah. [*Laughs*] Okay right, they're not going to get me like that . . . and . . . we're going out tonight . . . I'm taking you out tonight . . . you'll see us there, me and Graeme. I'll make sure of that. They're not going to make me look small, not in front of you . . . it's advertised and I'm going . . . we all are . . .

18   Pub

We are in the lounge of a public house where two models are moving a display of flowers. It is obviously a charity do. The **pub manager** *calls for quiet:* 'Order please'. *We see* **Graeme Souness** *and* **Sammy Lee**, *both men immaculately dressed and groomed, surrounded by 'well wishers'. The* **pub manager** *is between them.* **Lee** *and* **Souness** *are about to push over a huge, high pillar of pennies on a table in front of a crowd of photographers. Everyone is smiling and a roar goes up as the money scatters. As the audience cheer and applaud, the girls collect up the money and the media men take photos. Eventually the atmosphere settles down and people move away. There is standard pub-type piped music in the background throughout this scene. After signing a few autographs,* **Lee** *goes through the remnants of the crowd, followed by* **Souness**, *towards a table set out for them in a discreet corner. The manager's wife is already waiting there. They sit down. The* **manager** *takes a bottle out of a champagne bucket on the table and opens it. The cork pops. The manager's wife pours it. As we look on,* **Yosser** *goes past us towards the table. The* **manager** *is already twitching as* **Yosser** *goes to sit between the two footballers. There is not very much space. The* **manager** *is about to say something, when he looks out and sees something else that upsets him.* **Yosser** *turns to* **Lee**.

Yosser: Excuse me.

[*Footballers are used to head-bangers and* **Lee** *wryly gives him space. The* **pub manager** *finally speaks*]

Pub manager: Ah-hey Yosser, no kids allowed, know what I mean.

[*He points towards where the* **children** *are.* **Yosser** *stares malignantly at him*]

Manager: Well just this once, hey. Just for a few minutes.

[*Then nobody says anything. The footballers sip at the drink.* **Yosser** *turns slightly and looks at* **Souness**. **Souness** *looks at him, looks away and then has to look again*]

Yosser: You're Graeme Souness. Aren't you?

Souness: Yes.

Yosser: You're famous.

Souness: Well ...

Yosser: I'm Yosser Hughes. [*As if this explains everything*]

Souness: Pleased to meet you.

[**Yosser** *leans towards him, as if about to disclose a secret*]

Yosser: ... You look like me ...

Souness: Oh aye.

[**Yosser** *leans nearer still*]

Yosser: Magnum as well.

Souness: Pardon?

Yosser: Magnum. A detective. He used to be on the television. An American.

Souness: Oh aye.

[**Sammy Lee** *and the* **pub manager** *look on a bit bemused.* **Yosser** *drags a scrap of paper from his pocket.* **Sammy Lee** *looks at the two of them occasionally*]

Yosser: Sign this, for us will y' Graeme?

Souness: Sure. [*He takes hold of the paper, and gets a pen out*] Who's it for? [*He looks at the* **kids**]

Yosser: Me.

[*The* **kids** *smile*]

Souness: Erm ...

Yosser: Yosser Hughes.

[*His* **children** *look on. In an attempt to deflate the tension,* **Souness** *writes several words on the paper, then gives it back to* **Yosser** *who reads it*]

Yosser: 'To Yosser Hughes, better looking by far, best wishes, Graeme Souness.'

[**Yosser Hughes** *looks carefully at* **Souness**, *who shows no sign of irony*]

Yosser: Good that. Graeme.

[**Yosser** *looks away, past the camera, towards where his* **children** *and the other drinkers are. He is well pleased. Then he sits there, just facing out. There is a moment of terrible silence with all five facing out. The* **manager** *finally stands first, then his wife, quickly followed by both footballers. Quietly, with as little insult as possible, they begin to leave. Without looking at* **Yosser**, **Souness** *moves the champagne in front of him and then his own empty glass. They all walk away. We leave* **Yosser** *sitting there. He pours the champagne into a glass but doesn't drink it. He looks instead at the autograph in his hand, looks up and nods his head. Then he whispers the words to himself*]

Yosser: I could have been a footballer . . . but I had a paper round.

19 Yosser's house

A **man from the Electricity Board** *is knocking on* **Yosser's** *front door.* **Yosser** *opens the door and looks down from his front step.*

Electrician: Manweb.* I've come to turn off your power.

*Merseyside and North Wales Electricity Board

Yosser: Have y' got a good dentist?

Electrician: Ah come on, there's no need to threaten me, just close the door, that'll do me. All I have to do then is say I couldn't gain entry, and you've got two weeks grace. [*No answer*]

Electrician: Y' don't have to close the door if y' don't want. I'll lie about it.

[**Yosser** *moves off the step*]

Electrician: I hate this job y' know. I don't want to disconnect people. [*The* **electrician** *backs away towards his van. He coughs loud and false*] I've been off sick, they put me on this when I came back, I didn't ask for it . . . Look at me, I'm not that sort of person. [*He gets to the van, and opens the door*] But I tell you what though pal, if y' don't pay up, it gets nasty y' know. They bring men in. I'm just warning y', that's all.

[*As the van goes off, we see* **Yosser** *standing a yard or two from his front door staring out. Two more men approach, one of them a* **rent collector***, the other, with a briefcase attached to his left wrist, his minder.* **Yosser** *stares at him*]

Rent man: [*Almost in passing*] Morning Yosser, anything down for me? [*Nothing*] Not even a gesture of goodwill? [*Still nothing*] Fair enough, but a friendly warning. If y' don't pay y' rent, well, y' won't have any rent to pay, if y' know what I mean. [*Still nothing*] Don't say I didn't tell y'.

[*As the two men start to go off,* **Yosser** *takes hold of the minder's left arm. The minder looks down at* **Yosser's** *hand*]

Yosser: . . . Gizza job, go on, gizzit. I could do that. I can carry things. I've had practice.

[*The minder walks off.* **Yosser** *looks out*]

20   Yosser's house

A truck is parked up on the corner nearest **Yosser**'s *house.*
Maureen *is sitting in the cab with two men.* **Yosser** *and his*
children *leave the house and walk off. The* **children** *follow*
him, away from the truck. When **Yosser** *momentarily turns*
round, **Maureen** *and the two men lean back. She then looks*
out and indicates that they should approach the house. The
truck moves up the road.

21   Yosser's house

Two men load the personal possessions into the back of the
van.

22   Yosser's living room

The armchairs have already gone and the room is beginning to
look bare, especially as there wasn't that much anyway.
Maureen *is pacing the floor, quietly measuring the carpet. She*
glances briefly at some letters on the mantelpiece, all of them
formal. When the men return, one of them picks up a music
centre.

Maureen: No, don't take that, it isn't paid for yet. There's a
washing-machine and the fridge out there, but you can
forget the cooker, it's destroyed . . .

[*The removal man picks up the coffee table while the other*
one goes into the back kitchen and starts to move the
washing-machine. We see **Maureen** *look at a photograph of*
the children on the mantelpiece. She looks at it for a bit,
expressionless. But then she puts it face down before
throwing her house keys on the mantelpiece]

23   Yosser's living room

Now that the furniture has been removed the **boys** *have enough room to play football in the living room. That is just what they are doing. Meanwhile, the* **girl** *is drawing on the wall. Two people, a frail, bird-like* **woman** *and a* **young man***, knock on the open front door.*

Morgan: Hello.

[*They walk in, through the hall, and into the living room. The carpet has gone as well. All that's left are bare boards and a music centre. We see* **Yosser** *leaning his head on the wall above the mantelpiece, above where the gas fire used to be. He has hold of* **Maureen's** *house keys limply*]

Morgan: [*To the kids*] Hello lads, give us a kick, then, go on. [**Morgan** *knocks on the living room door*] Mr Hughes? Sorry, the door was open, er, we're from the Social Services, my name's Morgan —

[*As he speaks, the* **woman** *squats down in front of* **Yosser's** **daughter** *and smiles warmly*]

Veronica: Hello. I'm Veronica.

[**Yosser** *remains still and speaks quietly without looking round as if he has not heard the introductions being made*]

Yosser: I'm Yosser Hughes . . . This is my house, get out of my house.

[*When the* **children** *gather round* **Yosser***,* **Veronica** *crosses over to them and bends again*]

Veronica: And what's your name?

[*The* **children** *do not answer*]

Yosser: They're my children, they're staying with me. I'm

Yosser Hughes.

[*He stays where he is as the* **social workers** *exchange glances and look at the state of the room*]

24   Pier head

We see **Yosser**, *and then his* **children**, *against a background of the Liver Buildings at the pier head. He is amid the winos and derelicts on the benches, staring out, apparently unaware of everything around himself. His* **children** *are leaning over the railings, and they too reflect his vacancy. They are all becoming progressively more rough and dirty. Just above the noise of the crowd, we hear* **Yosser** *mumbling totally to himself at first.*

Yosser: It's all right, it's all right, it's all right though . . . I'm Yosser Hughes 'better looking by far'. [*He grins*] Everybody knows that. Everybody knows me. Everybody notices me. [*He turns to the* **wino** *sitting beside him*] You've noticed me, haven't you?

[**Yosser** *takes hold of the* **wino's** *arm as the* **wino** *lifts a bottle in a brown paper bag up to his lips. The* **wino** *is Scottish, in his fifties*]

Wino: Leave my disinfectant alone.

Yosser: I like to be noticed. Have you . . . noticed that? [**Yosser** *laughs at the lunacy of what he is saying. But he puts his hand back on the man's arm*]

Wino: I won't tell you again.

Yosser: Everywhere I go I get noticed. That's me.

[**Yosser** *keeps smiling and won't let go of his arm. The* **wino** *makes a half-hearted attempt to rid himself of* **Yosser**. *Then he stops*]

Wino: Are you . . . are you after my body?

[**Yosser** *seems to weigh the question up*]

Yosser: No. Everybody knows that. Everybody knows me. Graeme Souness knows me.

Wino: Souness, aye.

Yosser: I'm Yosser Hughes.

Wino: Listen, come on, listen to me. I want to tell you something.

Yosser: I know. I'm Yosser Hughes.

Wino: No listen, Jimmy.

Yosser: Yosser.

Wino: Yosser, they water this stuff down you know. They do. In the factory. I know, I have contacts. [*He taps his nose. He drinks from the bottle in the bag*] It's cold in this city, even in the summer. Eventually I shall migrate south for the winter . . . You can have my body if you want, I'm past caring.

[*Again we see the* **children** *leaning over the railings watching the ferries.* **Jason** *walks up and down.* **Yosser** *is still staring out front*]

Yosser: When I was little . . . when I was. There was so much to look forward to. Then. In the . . . in the fifties. When I was little. I built sandcastles.

[**Anne Marie** *comes to sit next to* **Yosser**. *When* **Yosser** *puts his arm around his daughter, the* **wino** *looks around slowly and absurdly to see if anyone is watching*]

Wino: Hey wait a minute.

[*The* **wino** *then pulls out from a pocket inside his overcoat a packet of Babycham chocolate liqueurs and holds them up to* **Yosser**. *Except that* **Yosser** *isn't looking*]

Wino: Thirty pence. Heh? Thirty. (*He looks at* **Yosser**.) Hey. You. For the little lady in your life.

[**Yosser** *turns towards the* **wino***, and takes hold of him by the lapels*]

Yosser: *I built sandcastles.* And ... I sometimes think that's all I've ever done.

[**Anne Marie** *has joined the other two at the railings again and they all three stare out*]

25   Interview room

We see **Maureen** *in close up. She is being interviewed. The whole delivery is documentary, perhaps almost like 'World in Action'. She is smoking heavily.*

Maureen: He hit me. A lot. All the time as a matter of fact. That's why I went out. But when I came back in, he'd hit me again. So I started not coming in at all. Look. I know it sounds awful, but it was him. He made me. [*There is a heavy pause. She feels that this isn't enough*] He was doing all kinds of daft things. He got this job in Saudi. And he made us move to this stupid big house. I don't know who he was trying to impress, but we couldn't possibly afford it. Then he lost his job. That really did send him down. And then, when they came knockin', it was then he started hittin' the kids. He did. He'd take it out on them. And he'd lock them in their bedroom at night. Without food ... I couldn't cope in the end. I had a sort of breakdown and I couldn't bear to be near him anymore. Or the kids. Because of what he'd done to me. And them. They didn't seem like mine anymore. That's why I don't want them now. They remind me. I'm sorry but I couldn't cope ... [*She leans forward*] If it's any help to you, I don't think they're his neither. I shouldn't say this, but there's a good chance they're not. When we were married I had this sort of friend ... Well. It was the only thing that kept me sane ...

You only have to look at them really. We've both got black hair, and the kids are blond . . . My friend was blond . . . he was a German sea-captain. You can use that, if you want. I'm going away anyway, he won't find me where I'm going . . . He wasn't very good, you know, he wasn't very good at anything. That was part of the trouble. He thought he was. And he always thought he was going to be somebody. [*She laughs*] And really he was nothing. [*She stares out*] Is that enough? [*We fade to black*]

26   Private house

We fade up from black to see **Yosser** *carrying a plastic bag of kittens, and each child carrying a kitten. Nearby, some builders are working in front of a house. We see* **George Malone** *stagger and fall on to a pile of sand.* **Yosser** *and the* **kids** *are trying and failing to sell kittens to the lady of the house. They leave with the owner following them into the drive and looking after them.* **Yosser** *and the* **kids** *approach the builders.*

Yosser: Wanna buy . . .

[*He and we see* **George**, *holding a spade, lying on a tip of sand, alongside of which are several bags of cement and bricks in piles of four hundred.* **George** *is dressed in a donkey jacket, pyjama bottoms and a pair of slippers. A brickie and his mate stare at* **George**, *unbelieving*]

Yosser: George? George.

[**Yosser** *drops the bag he is carrying. As the scene continues, several kittens crawl out of the bag and make their escape*]

Yosser: George, George!

[**Yosser** *picks* **George** *up off the sand*]

27 Hospital

We see **Yosser** *approaching the entrance gates to a hospital. We do not see for some time that* **Yosser** *is pushing* **George** *in a wheelbarrow. His* **children** *are straggling behind. It is, at first, as if* **Yosser** *is talking to himself.*

Yosser: Y'see George, it's the pressure. They're all after me. But if I was someone famous or y'know important, they wouldn't be. Am I right? If I was someone, they'd leave me alone. Y' don't stand a chance when y' no one, you've always said that an' you're spot on. They want my kids now. They've got everything else, now they want them as well. Listen, George, I can talk to you, George, you know everything, you're a great help to me . . . I'm not boring you, am I, George? George? Y' see, the thing is, I was all right when I was little, I was the king of the castle, but now I wet meself all the time . . . George, George, what am I going to do? . . . What, George?

[**George** *is plainly unconscious as* **Yosser** *takes him into the interior of the hospital*]

28 Catholic church

We see the interior light of a Roman Catholic church. It is almost empty, dimly lit and old-fashioned, full of candles, flowers, leaded windows and statues of the Virgin. Along one wall is a row of statues, each one with a plaque underneath it indicating one of the Stations of the Cross.

29 Confessional box

A **priest** *in his mid-thirties is sitting on his side of the Confessional in an old armchair. On the wall facing him is a square wood-framed grille with small curtains across it to*

*protect the identity of the guilty. On the small table by his chair
there are two books, 'A Book of Irish Wit and Humour' and 'For
Whom the Bell Tolls'. Alongside the books are a packet of
Bassett's Jelly Babies and an empty tea cup and saucer. The
priest has his eyes closed. As the door to the Confessional
opens, the* **priest** *opens his eyes and we hear someone shuffle in
on the sinner's side of the box. A second's silence, then, instead
of the expected sound of the door closing again, more feet are
heard. He hears the giggling of a group of* **children** *as they
come in.*

Priest: ... Yes? ... Hello?

[*The door finally closes. Someone kneels down. The* **priest**
*is slightly unnerved by the giggles and the knowledge that
there is a whole group of people out there*]

Priest: ... One at a time please. This isn't a spectator
sport!

[*He laughs a little but gets no reaction*]

Priest: Would you like to begin your confession?

[*The giggling continues. Then the* **children** *tell each other to
shut up, and settle down*]

Priest: Excuse me, excuse me. Would you like to start your
confession now? Thank you.

[*We can hear someone breathing, heavily but non-sexual.
The* **priest** *takes hold of the curtains and draws them back
fast.* **Yosser** *is framed by the square grille, with the light in
his side of the box directly above him. He is staring out,
facing the* **priest***, wild-eyed, both frightened and frightening.
Behind him, standing up by the door are his* **children***. The*
priest *pulls the curtain back across the grille*]

Priest: Oh! I'm sorry. I ... vandals, you know. You can
never be too ... I shouldn't really hear your confession in

the presence of anyone else, but the - er - children . . . your children? They're . . . if it's not a confession of any . . . consequence . . . er, turmoil.

[*There is still no answer, but the noise of the breathing increases. We hear a sobbing noise for a second*]

Priest: You . . . you do require confession, my son?

[**Yosser** *gives no answer, but continues sobbing as the* **priest***, who by now is genuinely aware of the man's condition, speaks*]

Priest: Do you want to talk to me, just . . . talk? You tell me . . .

[*But still there is no answer*]

Priest: Whatever you want, you tell me. That's what I'm here for. Through me, you can talk to . . .

[*The* **priest** *looks up at the heavens and begins to point as he talks, but decides against bringing God into this*]

Priest: . . . whoever might want to be listening. As it were. We are the guardians of the spirit, my son. Some kind of help in times of need . . .

[**Yosser** *finally stumbles out some words as we see the* **children** *quiet and listening*]

Yosser: Father, father . . . I'm . . . I'm . . .

Priest: Yes?

Yosser: I'm . . . I'm Yosser Hughes.

Priest: There's no need to tell me your . . .

Yosser: I'm desperate, father. Des . . . perate.

Priest: It can be a desperate world at times, Mr Hugh—

Yosser: Yosser Hughes.

Priest: It can be a desperate world at times yosserhughes. Tell me, if it makes it any easier . . .

[**Yosser** *is still sobbing. The* **priest** *goes again to take hold of the curtain, but stops. He talks over* **Yosser's** *sobs*]

Priest: A trouble shared in a place of peace, my son. A haven. I'm Father Thomas. 'Doubting' for short!

[*He opens the curtain again as he repeats the 'joke'*]

Priest: Doubting Thomas.

[**Yosser** *has his head resting against the grille, his hands clasped together, knuckles white*]

Priest: Daniel Thomas. I'm here to help you, yosserhughes. Daniel. Don't worry about the 'father'.

Yosser: I'm desperate, father.

[**Yosser** *looks up at the* **priest***, then closes his eyes*]

Priest: Call me Dan. Dan.

Yosser: I'm desperate. Dan.

[**Yosser** *looks up at the* **priest** *again. There is a fraction of a manic glance and he tries to laugh. Then he stops instantly. He seems to be screaming, silently as he leans back and then brings his head forward to butt the wooden frame surrounding the wire grille. The crucifix above drops down and hits him as he then butts and butts the wire grille*]

30   Hospital foyer

We see the entrance of a busy hospital. **Yosser** *and his three* **children** *walk in through the front door and go up the stairs.*

31   Doctor's consulting room, Psychiatric Unit

The consulting room is a bare white room with a waiting area/ hall outside. The furniture consists of a desk, a doctor's examining couch in one corner, and two chairs. A **lady** *in her late thirties is facing across the desk. Her face is severe.*

Anne Marie: I wanna go home, why can't we go home?

Doctor: I will not talk to you with your children present. It is as simple as that.

[**Yosser** *is sitting down in the* **doctor's** *room, with his* **children**, *whining and tetchy, in front of him, where he can see them, and in between him and the* **doctor**. *Sometimes he talks sanely and logically. Sometimes not*]

Yosser: Father Thomas did.

Doctor: I am not a priest, Mr Hughes.

Yosser: Just as well really. The Catholic Church has enough problems without women. [*He smiles*] Doctor.

[**Anne Marie** *whines throughout*]

Doctor: Take your children into the waiting area and I will talk to you. About your children for a start.

Yosser: No. They're staying where I can see them. It's a trick. They won't be there when I come out.

Doctor: Oh come on.

Yosser: It's true.

Doctor: Ah yes, the conspiracy theory. The whole world is against you.

Yosser: That's not true. But you don't like me, do you?

Doctor: That's neither here nor —

Yosser: Nobody likes me.

Doctor: Take your children outside and we can talk.

Yosser: No chance.

Doctor: Leave the door open so that you can see them.

Yosser: Someone'll snatch them. Someone'll lock the door from the outside and they'll be gone. And when that happens, you're dead.

Doctor: [*Gently*] Please take your children outside, and if you won't do that, please take yourself outside.

Yosser: [*Peering between his* **children**] I'm Yosser Hughes.

Doctor: Mr Hughes, you are putting yourself, your children and the parental custody of your children at risk by your behaviour.

Yosser: Don't talk like that in front of my children.

[*The frenzied pace drops for a space and* **Yosser** *leans forward*]

Yosser: Look, I only came here 'cos I had to. I'm not cracked. There's nothing wrong with me. I'm Yosser Hughes.

Doctor: Goodbye, Mr Hughes.

[*She goes to write in the case book she has in front of her.* **Yosser** *stands up, goes to the door with his* **children**, *opens the door and looks out into the waiting area. Then he moves a few yards out of the office with the* **children** *and places them where he can see them. They stand there, not moving.* **Yosser** *backs in to the* **doctor**, *and stands at the far corner of her desk, not looking at her at all, staring out of the door*]

Yosser: Why? Why?

Doctor: Mr Hughes, you have to face facts. Your wife does not want to see you anymore.

Yosser: But why? Why?

Doctor: Surely the events speak for themselves?

Yosser: They haven't talked to me.

Doctor: Possibly because you won't listen. [*The* **doctor** *becomes more gentle*] This is getting us nowhere. Please either sit down and discuss this matter or ... leave the room.

[**Yosser** *promptly sits on the side of her desk, his back to her, still looking out towards the waiting area*]

Doctor: You cannot condone what you have done, Mr Hughes. You have attacked your wife. And her ... associates. Physically attacked them.

Yosser: I was provoked.

Doctor: Physically?

Yosser: Mental's worse. [**Yosser** *looks at her for the first time since he came back into the room. And leans on her desk*] You'd support that argument wouldn't you? [*Grins and then stops*] You know why you're called a shrink, don't y'? 'Cos y' shrink people — that's what y' tryin' to do to me — but y' won't an' y' know why — 'cos I'm Yosser Huges, y' won't shrink me. She tried that, she used to shrink everythin'. One wash and there it was — fit for a midget. [*He laughs and stops*] I want her back. [*He is still looking at her*]

Doctor: ... But she isn't coming back.

Yosser: I don't really want her back.

Doctor: Well then.

Yosser: I just want her there.

Doctor: [*Gently*] I feel just like that sometimes. About my three-piece suite.

[**Yosser** *sits down at last*]

Yosser: She's not coming back, is she?

Doctor: I don't think so.

Yosser: That's all right. All she ever did was frig off. She never cooked for me or nothin'. She didn't love me. She didn't love the kids. I know you want to talk to me about the kids. I want to keep the kids.

[*No answer*]

Yosser: I want to keep the kids.

[*He looks away towards the* **kids** *but they aren't there in the doorway. He virtually leaps off the chair towards the chair and goes flying out of the door in total panic. He runs up and down the waiting area outside her office in mounting panic*]

32   Lifts at Day Clinic

He runs down the corridor, and then sees the three **children** *just a couple of yards away at the lift doorway. The eldest has his hand near the button. The lift door is open.* **Yosser** *dives for the lift, expecting to see the kidnappers in there. But he cannot see into the lift until he enters it at a great pace, ready to kill. There is nobody there at all. He looks at his* **children** *with desperate anxiety, and goes down on his knees. The* **doctor** *follows down the corridor. The eldest presses the lift button just as the doors are beginning to close on* **Yosser***. He tries to get up off his knees to the door.*

Jason: We were just . . .

[*And as the doors close, the* **doctor** *joins* **Yosser's children** *outside the lift*]

Yosser: Let me out. It's a trap. Anne Marie, stay there. Dustin, don't go with them. Stay there, Jason.

Doctor: Mr Hughes. It's all right, they're with me.

[**Yosser** *presses a button. We hear* **Yosser** *going away*]

Yosser: Stay there, stay there . . .

[*The lift starts to go to the ground floor. The lift doors open on
to the ground floor foyer, then close again. The* **doctor**
kneels down on her haunches to **Yosser's** **children**. *We see
that they appear tired, withdrawn and distant, as well as
dirt-stained. Only their eyes, constantly looking around, give
any sign of emotion or nervousness*]

Doctor: Are you all right?

[*They all nod*]

Doctor: Are you sure?

[*We hear the sound of* **Yosser** *butting the instrument panel
as the lift returns and the doors open again. At an angle, we
see* **Yosser** *at the side of the lift interior. Butting the
instrument panel. He is crying*]

Yosser: Don't touch them, leave them alone . . . Don't
touch 'em.

[*And the doors close again on him. He makes no attempt to
stop them from shutting*]

33   Yosser's bedroom

The **children** *are in their pyjamas on the double bed.* **Anne
Marie** *is singing 'All Things Bright and Beautiful' while the
boys are reading magazines and drawing.*

Jason: Shut up, Anne Marie.

[*She whispers the words, gradually getting back to singing it
again.* **Yosser** *comes through the doorway looks in on his*
children, *ruffles* **Dustin's** *hair and sits down on the single
bed*]

Yosser: ... When you were born y' know, when you were born... I mean, when you were born. Then it was... it was ... I was all right then. Without me you ... But I didn't know then. You don't know. You never know. You think you do, but you don't.

[Inevitably they are not listening to him. Even if they were, they wouldn't understand what he is talking about. **Yosser** *goes to them and lies down on the double bed. The youngest lies down beside him and cuddles his father]*

34   Yosser's living room

The **two people from the Social Services Department** *are back again, gently, patiently trying to explain it all to* **Yosser**.

Morgan: Mr Hughes, I'm sorry but we do have authority under the Children's Act and Young People's Act of 1969 to remove your children regardless of your permission or not.

Veronica: We only want them to receive proper care, Mr Hughes.

[We see **Yosser** *from a few yards away. He lifts the small bird-like social worker up by her coat, revealing his unacceptable side, with trumps. The* **lady** *is dangling between* **Yosser** *and the* **other social worker** *who is behind her]*

Yosser: Care? Care? What do you care. You can't care for them like I care for them.

*[***Yosser** *drops the* **lady social worker** *and pushes her away on to the* **male social worker's** *feet. When the back of her head hits the* **male social worker** *in the face, he doesn't know whether to limp or have a nosebleed]*

Veronica: [*To* **Morgan**] Are you all right?

Yosser: I'm sorry. No, sorry. Sorry.

[*He touches her lapels*]

Yosser: . . . You'd better go away.

Veronica: Calm down, Mr Hughes.

Yosser: No, you better had. I'm caring for them. There's no need for a place of safety. They've got me . . .

[*He pursues them down the hall*]

Yosser: . . . 'Cos listen, you can summons me to see a magistrate till life everlasting. I'm not goin'. There's no one in need here. Listen, I'm telling you, and you'd better believe me, don't come back unless you bring an army.

[**Yosser** *is at the front door and* **Morgan** *and* **Veronica** *are running into the road.* **Yosser** *slams the door*]

35   Yosser's house

The army **Yosser** *was talking about has arrived and are waiting patiently, for the inevitable. The* **two social workers** *are knocking at the downstairs window of* **Yosser***'s house. One of them is waving a 'Place of Safety Order'. They call as they knock.*

Morgan: Mr Hughes.

Veronica: Mr Hughes.

Morgan: It's Morgan and Veronica from the Social Services, Mr Hughes.

Veronica: Please come out, Mr Hughes.

Morgan: Please, Mr Hughes, just a quick word.

Veronica: Mr Hughes. If you'd just come to the door, Mr Hughes.

[*A **third social worker** knocks on the door and keeps knocking and knocking. A Social Services mini-bus is parked a little way down the road with three or four men inside. One of the social workers crosses over to a police car which is parked alongside it, full of policemen. A small crowd is gathering at the edges of the scene*]

Social worker: We can handle this ourselves, we don't need you, we just need a bit more time.

[*We do not see **Yosser** or the **children. Morgan** and **Veronica** are still trying to raise **Yosser**, when they are joined by the **driver of the police car**. He has a large half-circle scar on his face*]

Scarface policeman: You're new at this job, aren't y', love?

Veronica: Yes, but I don't see what that's got to do with . . .

Scarface policeman: How old are you — sixteen, seventeen?

Morgan: Hey now, just hold on pal.

Scarface policeman: Leave it to me, all right? Otherwise we'll be here all day. [*He begins to walk away*] Y' don't get anywhere bein' pleasant to shite.

[*He goes to the car and gets the other three policemen out*]

Scarface policeman: Andy, you go by the front door, the rest of you round the back with me.

[*The **social workers** at the window resume knocking and calling and looking into the living room*]

Moss: Mr Hughes!

Veronica: Mr Hughes!

Morgan: I think it'd be better if you did come out now, Mr Hughes.

Veronica: Mr Hughes!

[*As the three policemen run round the back, a policeman and dog get out of a police van and wait*]

Morgan: Mr Hughes, please, Mr Hughes!

[*They are knocking even more frantically*]

36   Back yard/back kitchen/living room

The **policemen** *kick the back gate and smash the glass in the back door. They unbolt the door and they are in.* **Yosser** *appears from the shadowy light in the hall, and runs down the stairs, wielding a baseball bat. He confronts the* **policeman** *in the kitchen.*

Scarface policeman: Put it down you bastard!

[*The three policemen now have their truncheons drawn. It is Cowboys and Indians time.* **Yosser** *takes one swing with the bat, but is hit from all sides. And hit and hit until he falls down.* **Yosser** *attempts to fight back but he doesn't stand a chance.* **Veronica** *and* **Morgan** *can only watch helplessly through the window.* **Scarface** *watches with a smirk on his face*]

37   Yosser's house

At the end of this beating, **Veronica** *turns away from the window, and looks straight out, facing us with a shocked and sickened look on her face.* **Scarface** *walks from the living room into the hall followed by the other policemen. He is obviously well pleased with his day's work.* **Morgan** *and* **Veronica** *are on their way in.*

Scarface policeman: They're all yours. They're under the bed upstairs.

Veronica: Well, you bastard!

[*They go inside and up the stairs.* **Scarface** *grins happily at her, and then he and his companions walk back to the car, strutting big men. Until a single airgun shot rings out, and* **Scarface** *howls, holding his backside*]

Scarface policeman: I've been shot, I've been shot!

[**Scarface** *and the other three policemen dive out of sight behind their cars. Now we see a* **boy** *in a first-floor window with an airgun firing determinedly at them. They are trapped behind their cars as more shots are fired and more ducking follows*]

[*We see the* **lad with the air gun** *being dragged out of his house by the* **policeman** *and bundled into the police car. We faintly hear his solitary protest*]

Scarface policeman: Come on.

Boy with airgun: But I'm a hero . . .

Scarface: Shut up.

38   Yosser's house

We come back as **Yosser's children** *are being brought down the stairs from the bedroom and out of the house.* **Morgan** *and a* **male social worker** *are carrying a boy each, and* **Veronica** *has hold of the daughter. All three* **children** *are screaming and resisting care. Wildly. We see* **Yosser** *lying still on the floor.*

Kids: No, no, no what about my dad? Dad! Put me down! Dad!

Veronica: Your daddy is going to be all right, Anne Marie.

Kids: No! No!

Morgan: It's all right, you're going to see your daddy soon, it's all right.

Anne Marie: Dad!

Veronica: It's all right.

[*We focus on* **Veronica** *and* **Anne Marie**. **Veronica** *is carrying the girl, and holding her wrists to stop her from fighting. The girl stops struggling as they get to the mini van and she stares at* **Veronica** *for a second.* **Veronica** *smiles at her reassuringly. The smile is returned. Happiness is restored. Then* **Anne Marie** *butts her in the face.* **Veronica** *squeals*]

Veronica: Ooh you little . . .

[**Anne Marie** *looks well pleased*]

39 Yosser's living room

We pan around the empty living room onto **Yosser** *who is sitting huddled in a corner, with four days' growth of beard. He is wearing his overcoat, and has two empty milk bottles at his side, as well as two packets of cornflakes, the remnants of a sliced loaf, a tub of margarine, an empty tin of spam, and a knife. He also has a black eye, the bruising well out and flourishing. We hold on him. He stares out. It is as if he has stared out for days, but then, as we hold, some animation comes into his face. He starts to nod his head slightly, as if he had reached a decision. He begins to struggle to his feet. A floorboard creaks.*

40   Hospital

The **woman psychiatrist** *is in her room with a* **black female patient** *who is smoking heavily.*

Doctor: How many do you think you need?

Hospital patient: Well, four a day, but I need more on Sunda—

[*The* **doctor'***s door bursts open and* **Yosser** *enters as if he has just finished running a four-minute mile. He stands a few yards into the room, out of breath and shaking*]

Yosser: Where are they — WHERE ARE THEY? I've been looking for them but I can't find them. I couldn't even find you. Where are they? You know, you must know, you put them away. You must know where they are. Where are they?

[*He turns and leans against the wall, head first, back turned. His pose has as much exhaustion in it as pleading*]

Doctor: Mr Hughes, to be absolutely honest, in all truth . . .

Yosser: Yeah, they all start like that and then they tell me lies. Where are they? I've been everywhere looking for them. I've been to Bellevale and Marsh Lane —

Hospital patient: [*Flatly*] That's where mine are.

Yosser: I've been to the Cenocle and Mount Pleasant —

Hospital patient: Excuse me —

Yosser: I can't find them anywhere. Where are they?

Hospital patient: Excuse me, but this is my appointment. It took me three buses to get here, and you only get a quarter of an hour anyway.

Doctor: If you would just wait outside, Mr Hughes.

Yosser: No!

[*He collapses onto the floor by the wall*]

Doctor: Please.

Hospital patient: This isn't fair, you know. And there's a queue.

Doctor: Please wait outside, Mr Hughes.

Yosser: Put me away, hey?

[*He get up and crawls to lean on the edge of her desk, pleading, but with suppressed rage*]

Yosser: Send me away. Where are they? Let me be with them. WHERE ARE THEY? Let me be with them. Mm? Put me away too. Mm? I can be with them . . . I can be with them.

[**Yosser** *looks up at the* **doctor***, puts his index finger up to his bottom lip, and flicks at his lip, making blubbering noises like a child. He tries to smile, but it descends quickly to tears, then to solid, pained weeping. His body shaking, near to convulsion, he huddles into the corner, hands over his head. The* **female patient** *watches him, becoming just ever so slightly alarmed. The* **doctor** *picks up her phone and begins dialling*]

Hospital patient: What . . . what's he doing that for?

Doctor: Penance . . .

[*We leave on* **Yosser's** *huddled weeping*]

41   Yosser's house

Two men stack plywood against the railing outside **Yosser's** *house, and then go to join a third man with an official-looking piece of paper who is leaning against a car. They wait until they, and we, see* **Yosser** *come slowly down the street and go into his house. The* **man with the paper** *goes to him.*

Eviction man: I'm sorry about this, sir, it's an eviction order, and we'd like as little fuss as possible please. For your own good.

Yosser: Have it, go on, have it. May you always be . . .

[**Yosser** *goes inside the house as the* **eviction man** *gestures to the men, who go and start nailing the plywood across the windows*]

42 Yosser's house

We see one of the men knocking the final plywood into place across a window. What little stuff was left in the house has been piled spreadeagled in the street. **Yosser** *comes out of the front door and starts walking away past the furniture. He is holding limply at his side the photograph of his children that was on the mantelpiece. As he passes the men and the plywood, he has a last, desperate attempt.*

Yosser: . . . I could do that . . .

[*As he goes, he takes the photograph from its frame, throws the frame on to the pile of furniture, and walks away clutching the photograph*]

43 Williamson Square; early morning

It is the early hours of the morning. There is heavy rain. Apart from **Yosser** *sitting on a bench, soaked, and looking like a tramp, Williamson Square is deserted. We see another figure approaching from Whitechapel. He sits down next to* **Yosser**. *It is the Scottish* **wino**.

Wino: Lend me ten shillings. I need ten shillings for shoes. I'll get you a pair as well. I'll come back with them. [*He looks at* **Yosser** *for the first time*] Don't I know you from somewhere?

Yosser: I'm . . . I'm . . . I'm wet.

Wino: It's the climate son.

Yosser: I wish I was dead.

Wino: It's this city, man. Naw, if I had decent shoes I'd be awa'. F. off, vamoos [*Pause*] I'm not sitting here much longer, I can tell you. It's all wet. [*Pause*] Have you got a brick?

Yosser: Not on me, no.

[*He shows the* **wino** *the photograph*]

Yosser: If you see these on your travels, will you tell me?

Wino: They won't be where I'm going, pal. I'm going somewhere dry. I'm gonna travel.

[*He gets up and moves to a shop window*]

Yosser: They won't be in there.

Wino: If you break a window you get a cell for the night. You get the evening as well. It's warm in a cell, and there's nae mair rain.

[*He starts to sing and dance and kick at the window. He is joined by* **Yosser** *who has fetched a barrel from outside the pub next door.* **Yosser** *hurls the barrel straight through the window*]

Wino: That was my window.

[*They hear the alarm go off and are helpless to do anything except wait*]

44　Williamson Square

There is now a police car in the Square, its blue light revolving. The **police driver** *is smoking a cigarette. We hear, then see,* *the **other policeman** in front of the broken window and between **Yosser** and the **wino**. They are all talking at once.*

Wino: It was me.

Yosser: No it wasn't, it was me.

Wino: It wasn't, it was me. I did it. You caught me before I could get away.

Yosser: It was me.

Policeman: [*To* **Yosser**] Look, do me a favour — piss off. I know it's him, he's always at it. [*Turns to the* **wino**] Come ahead, Jock . . .

[**Yosser** *takes hold of the* **policeman**]

Yosser: But it wasn't, it was me.

[*The* **policeman** *shoves him away. The* **policeman** *takes hold of the* **wino** *and pushes him towards the car*]

Yosser: But . . .

[**Yosser** *begins to follow them*]

Yosser: But . . .

[*He takes hold of the* **policeman's** *free arm but the* **policeman** *jerks away*]

Yosser: But . . .

[*They reach the police car. The* **policeman** *turns as* **Yosser** *takes hold of him again*]

Yosser: But . . .

Policeman: Hey — don't 'but' me, all right?

[*We see a mad smile on* **Yosser's** *face. We leave the scene as he moves his head back*]

45   A police car

The **policeman** *who has just been butted is holding a handkerchief to his nose. The handkerchief is blood-stained and he has had a heavy nosebleed. His* **colleague** *is driving. The* **wino** *is singing again.*

Policeman: Shut it.

> [*The* **wino** *stops singing and the* **policeman** *turns to* **Yosser** *speaking through his handkerchief*]

Policeman: You're dead you are, I'm tellin' y', dead.

> [**Yosser** *turns to the* **wino**]

Yosser: I'm dead . . . I said I'm dead.

Wino: [*Not looking*] Good. I'm glad.

Yosser: So am I. I'm dead . . . but you smell.

Wino: I know.

Yosser: That's all right then. [*He leans forward towards the* **policeman**] Why am I dead?

Policeman: You'll find out when I get you back to the station, now just shut up.

> [*He is called up on the mobile radio telephone*]

Voice: Alpha Tango 23.

Policeman: Alpha Tango 23. Go ahead.

Voice: Alpha Tango 23, report of demonstration and possible riot at Aigburn Drive, Sefton Park area. Please investigate.

Policeman: Alpha Tango 23. We're on our way. [*Puts receiver down*]

> [*The police car approaches Sefton Park with its siren going. It slows and the siren stops. We hear the* **policeman's** *voice*]

Policeman: Riots? What riots? Four old women with four old dogs, three flashers, five million bloody joggers and two head-bangers in the back. Alpha Tango 23 over and out. [*He slams the receiver down*]

Yosser: I though I knew where I was going once. I did. But there's nowhere left to go. 'Cos it's all . . .

Wino: Gone.

[**Yosser** *turns on him*]

Yosser: This is my conversation.

[*He turns back, the* **wino** *mumbles*]

Wino: . . . I hate Scousers.

Yosser: All right, I know it's my fault. I know I'm to blame. I know that. I know that much. But what I want to know is — is this all there is? Down to this. For the rest of my life. Hey? Hey? Hey? Hey?

[*The* **policeman** *half turns and pushes* **Yosser** *backwards knocking him on to the seat.* **Yosser** *makes no attempt to retaliate, but sits back in the seat. He talks to himself and the others let him*]

Yosser: Not me. No chance. There's nothing down for me — and I'm not staying around for that. The trouble is most of us either talk to ourselves or through our arse. I've found that out. I'm thirty-six years old and I've found that out . . . Unless you're somebody. Somebody. And I bet it's crap for them an' all. I bet Graeme Souness is really unhappy.

[*There is a pause.* **Yosser** *scowls*]

Yosser: I bet.

[*The* **policeman** *who was butted is still blowing his nose tenderly.* **Yosser** *sees something out of the window. As the car approaches the lake in Sefton Park,* **Yosser** *looks at the*

policemen, *half smiles then stops*]

Yosser: I'm going to be sick.

Policeman: Oh shite . . .

Yosser: Very . . . sick.

Policeman: Not in here y' not.

[*He gestures to the* **driver** *and the police car slams to a halt. The* **policeman** *proceeds to drag* **Yosser** *out of the back of the car with* **Yosser** *talking all the while as he is bundled out and led to the side of the road*]

Yosser: Everything I've ever wanted, and all the things that I thought I had, they've all been taken away. I've got to take something. It's my turn.

[*The* **policeman** *pushes* **Yosser** *and gets hold of him by the back of the neck*]

Policeman: Just get on with it, will y'.

[*He tries to push* **Yosser** *into a 'sick' position.* **Yosser** *straightens up and shakes his head*]

Yosser: I'm Yosser Hughes. And I can't stand it anymore.

[**Yosser** *charges off towards the lake. The* **policeman** *follows him. The* **driver** *gets out, stops and shouts into the car*]

Police driver: You stay there.

[*As the* **driver** *joins the chase, the* **wino** *answers*]

Wino: Where else would I be going?

[*They both chase after* **Yosser** *who is hurtling towards the lake. The* **policeman** *is close behind him, but stops as* **Yosser** *goes crashing straight into the water and then on and on into the lake. The* **police driver** *finally catches up. They both stand on the edge of the water, bewildered. We see*

Yosser *swimming wildly towards the centre of the lake. He stops and treads water. Then he hurls himself under the water. He emerges. We see the two* **policemen** *on the edge*]

Police driver: He's ...

Policeman: Let the bastard die.

[*We go back to* **Yosser** *who hurls himself under the water for a second time, and for longer. He emerges spewing water*]

Yosser: [*Howling*] Come on, come on ...

[*When he goes down again, we hold for a long time and still there is no sign. We go back to the* **policemen**. *They look at each other*]

Police driver: Nah ...

[*The* **driver** *starts taking his jacket off, the other one hesitates and then starts hurtling his jacket off in a tantrum.* **Yosser** *comes up and is visibly upset about the fact. He hurls himself down again, and this time stays down. From a distance we see the* **driver**, *followed by the* **other policeman**, *reaching the spot where* **Yosser** *was. The* **driver** *dives down, comes up and dives again. The* **other policeman** *paddles about. The* **driver** *comes back up, holding* **Yosser** *by his jacket, half loses him, then gets him again. Between them they start bringing* **Yosser** *towards shore,* **Yosser** *like a dead weight.* **Yosser** *is being hauled out of the lake. The two* **policemen** *go down on their knees.* **Yosser** *who is lying on his stomach appears unconscious or dead. The* **policemen** *get off their knees and pummel him desperately to resuscitate him. They go about their task with dedication, and in* **Nosebleed's** *case, physical violence. Eventually,* **Yosser** *opens his eyes. And finally he lifts his head and begins howling*]

Yosser: No no no. NO!

[The final 'NO' is howled and reverberated. We freeze frame on his face, then zoom in tight on to his eye. Freeze. Silence then music]

George's Last Ride

First shown on BBC2 on 7 November 1982

Characters

George Malone
Chrissie Todd
Yosser Hughes
Loggo Logmond
Dixie Dean
Kevin Dean
Mrs Malone, George's wife
Ritchie Malone ⎫
John Malone ⎭ George's sons (in their thirties)
George's grandchildren
Hospital doctor
Family doctor
Priest
DoE clerk
Pub Manager
Shake-hands
Glass collector
'Ronny Renaldo'
Gnasher Llewellyn
Redundancy party
Youths in pub

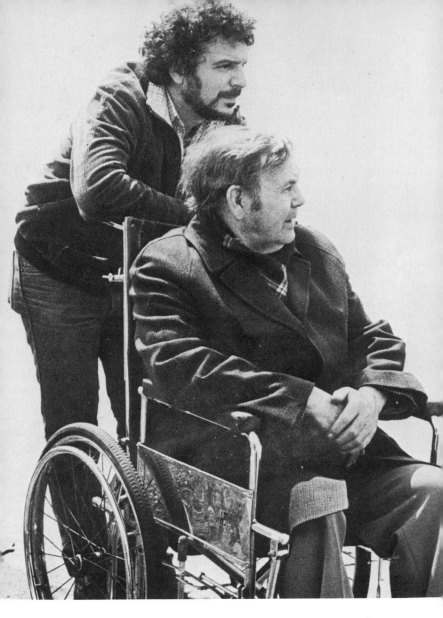

Michael Angelis as Chrissie and Peter Kerrigan as George in George's Last Ride

George's Last Ride

---

1   Department of Employment

We see the exterior of the DoE.

2   Department of Employment; main hall

We see **George** *at the counter of the DoE. Then the* **female clerk's** *face. She is concerned, but barely able to look out front for more than a second.* **George** *is in cheerful mood.*

George: Are you trying to tell me something, lass?

Clerk: . . . Mr Malone, you're wearing pyjamas. Again.

[*We see* **George**. *He doesn't look as though he is wearing pyjamas. He looks down at his jacket and feels it. Then he looks at the* **clerk**]

Clerk: Pyjama bottoms.

George: That's my jogging gear.

Clerk: You'll catch you — you'll catch a cold like this. You know you will. Please Mr Malone, you know you shouldn't be here. Let me —

George: It's the tablets girl. They do your head in. I'm not gonna take them anymore.

[*She goes to the phone. He follows her to the grille*]

George: Ah no, don't call an ambulance, girl. [*He begins to back away*] I'm going home, they're not going to stop me. But if it makes you happy, I'll go back to the hospital first.

[**George** *walks away and goes through the doors. The* **clerk** *moves back to her position, then stands up and goes out after him. We see he is wearing pyjamas beneath his working jacket*]

3   Department of Employment

Dixie *and* **Kevin** *approach along the pavement. They go up the steps and meet the* **counter-clerk** *who is coming out.*

Clerk: Excuse me, you haven't seen an old feller in pyjamas, have you?

Dixie: Yeah I saw him. He went down there, what's more he was riding a camel and carrying a handbag. You saw him, didn't you Kev?

Kevin: Yeah I saw him.

Clerk: Seriously.

Dixie: [*Over his shoulder*] Are you going off your rocker behind that counter?

Clerk: George Malone.

Dixie: George? But he's in hospital isn't he?

Clerk: He was, but he's just walked out of here wearing pyjamas.

Dixie: You're joking?

Clerk: I'm not.

[*The* **clerk**, **Dixie** *and* **Kevin** *walk down the steps to look for* **George**]

Dixie: You're sure it's George?

Clerk: *Yes*. George Malone.

Dixie: Which way did he go?

Clerk: I don't know.

[*And they walk along the pavement*]

Dixie: [*To a passer-by*] You haven't seen George Malone have you?

4 Albert Docks

We see **George's** *feet and pyjama-clad legs. He coughs, and we see* **George's** *face, and then* **George's** *hand guiding himself down the steps, and along the edge of the dock.*

Ritchie's *wagon approaches.* **Ritchie** *is driving and* **John** *is sitting next to him, with* **Chrissie** *and* **Loggo** *in the back of the wagon riding 'shotgun'. The van comes to a stop. We see* **George** *approach an old capstan. We hear* **Loggo** *and* **Chrissie** *talking over this action.*

Loggo: How did you know he'd be here?

[**Chrissie** *laughs*]

Chrissie: He spends more time here now than when he used to work here.

[**George** *turns an old wheel and then looks up to see the van.* **Ritchie** *and* **John** *are walking towards him*]

Ritchie: Dad ... dad ... dad. Y' not supposed to be here.

5 Hospital

Ritchie's *wagon passes the Walton Hospital sign and turns into the hospital grounds. When the van stops,* **John** *gets out.*

Then **George** *struggles out of the van and is helped towards the entrance by* **Ritchie** *and* **John**.

6   Hospital ward

The nurse walks into the ward towards **George Malone** *who is in a hospital bed, propped up on a pillow and now wearing a complete and matching set of pyjamas, top and bottom. He is trying to look well, confident and cheerful. But we can see that the bed next to his, nearest the ward door, is empty. A* **doctor** *who is in his mid-thirties and who has a closed file in his hands is with him. He also speaks with a surprisingly strong Liverpool 'rough and ready' accent.*

Doctor: Anyway, you should be taking advantage of the rest, Mr Malone.

George: [*Coughs*] I don't like hospitals, doctor. It's as simple as that. It's a tradition in our family, when y' went in hospital you were as good as dead.

Doctor: Oh rubbish.

George: Especially when they put you in a bed near the corridor.

Doctor: It's an understandable fear, Mr Malone, but those days are long gone.

George: Try tellin' that to the feller who was in the next bed. You'd need a loudhailer though.

[*Another patient laughs. The* **doctor** *looks at the laughing man then goes back to* **George**]

Doctor: Mr James was extremely ill, and besides you really shouldn't be so pessimistic.

George: I'm not being pessimistic, I just want to go home. I felt great today and I've got a bit of work to do.

Doctor: Absolutely impossible.

George: All right, I want to go out for a walk then.

Doctor: Mr Malone, you went for a walk yesterday, and —

George: Twice.

Doctor: Yes, twice, and the second time an ambulance had to bring you back.

George: They didn't give me a chance to get my second wind.

Doctor: I must insist.

George: And hiding my clothes is not going to make any difference, either, Sister.

Doctor: Oh . . . Mr Malone, you are not a healthy man. At the moment.

George: There you are then. Let me go home before I die.

Doctor: You're not going to die.

George: Oh? Immortality as well. That's a good offer, doctor. Considering I'm on the National Health.

[**George** *grins at the* **doctor**]

Doctor: All right, listen to me. You've had surgery, right? From which it takes time to recover. You may need further surgery, I don't know. No one will know until we hear the results of the tests. And you can't expect to go back to work straightaway. The only thing your body wants at the moment is complete rest and recuperation. Surely you understand that?

George: And I'm not taking any more of those head-banging tablets, Sister.

Doctor: I don't believe this, you really are an old sod, aren't you?

George: Yes. [**George** *leans forward. He points*] 'Do not go gentle into that good night, Old age should burn and rave at close of day.'

Doctor: 'Rage, rage against the dying of the light.'

George/Doctor: Dylan Thomas.

Doctor: 'Though wise men at their end know dark is right, Because their works have forked no lightning, they . . .'

George: All right, smart arse.

Doctor: 'Do not go gentle.'

[*The* **doctor** *stands, ruffles* **George's** *hair, laughs 'good night' then turns away.* **George** *talks as they move*]

George: And what's more the food's a disgrace.

[*The* **doctor** *laughs harder. The Sister follows him out*]

7   Sister's office

The **doctor** *and the Sister come into her room. There is a pause. The* **doctor** *sits by the window, then speaks tonelessly.*

Doctor: I lied to him, Sister. The results came through this morning.

[*The Sister looks at him*]

Doctor: Goodnight and God Bless. [*He pauses again*] Oh shit and derision. Sometimes I wish I was a vet. [*He walks out, as he finishes talking*] I'm terribly sorry to tell you this, Mrs Malone, but your dormouse is dying . . .

[*The* **doctor** *and Sister leave the room*]

8   Hospital consulting room

The **doctor** *sits facing* **Mrs Malone** *in a small consulting room* *in the hospital. Like* **George**, *she is in her early sixties. But she is well, well-preserved, and well-dressed, without a trace of blue rinse or country life.*

Doctor: I would therefore suggest, in fact I would strongly recommend, that more radical surgery should at least be considered.

Mrs Malone: He doesn't want that. Doctor.

Doctor: It's not always a complete waste of . . . time. It can very often give time.

Mrs Malone: He wants to go home.

Doctor: Yes I understand that. [*Pause*] Are you going to tell him.

Mrs Malone: [*Quietly*] Surely it's obvious.

Doctor: . . . Pardon?

Mrs Malone: He already knows. That's why he wants to go home.

Doctor: [*Pause*] He keeps going on about his 'work', Mrs Malone. But obviously he can never return to work.

Mrs Malone: He hasn't worked in eighteen months.

Doctor: Oh good. That's fine.

[*When she looks at him, the* **doctor** *hesitates again*]

Doctor: No—er— I'm sorry. I mean it's . . . this is perhaps somewhat silly. [*He laughs nervously*] But I—er— my father worked on the docks, Mrs Malone, and he was somewhat of a militant but there was a man there, he was the chairman of the shop stewards' committee. I went to a meeting he chaired once — my father took me, rather he made me go — I was only a boy at the time, eleven or twelve. It's twenty-five or maybe thirty years ago you understand. [*He stumbles to a halt*]

Mrs Malone: Yes, go on.

Doctor: Well this man's name was George Malone and the people in the hall kept chanting for him to speak, kept on and on till he did . . . I'm sorry. I just wondered if it was possibly the same person.

Mrs Malone: Oh aye, it's the same person. He was blacklisted in '58 and went to work on the blackstuff.

Doctor: The blackstuff?

Mrs Malone: The tarmac.

Doctor: Ah. The tarmac. Yes, well. I listened to him speak that night . . . like I'd never heard anyone speak before . . . or since. Of . . . one for all, and all for one. With the most tremendous passion . . .

Mrs Malone: Aye that's him.

Doctor: I've never forgotten it . . . My father spoke about him a lot. He said he was a great man.

Mrs Malone: He still is, doctor.

Doctor: Yes he still is. [*He turns away from her*] Would you like to come through?

[*She nods, they rise and move towards the door.* **Mrs Malone** *speaks as they get outside the door*]

Mrs Malone: Do you have any political beliefs, doctor?

Doctor: Well yes, actually, I'm — er — very involved with the local Liberal Party. And the SDP, of course. [*He laughs*] The Alliance, you know.

Mrs Malone: [*Lightly*] Listening to my husband didn't really have that much effect then, after all?

[*She walks away*]

[*We see the* **doctor's** *reaction*]

9   Hospital ward

A nurse is looking out of the open window. She shouts 'Mr Malone'. Then she goes to **George's** *empty bed where* **Mrs Malone** *joins her.*

Mrs Malone: Oh God!

Doctor: Oh, no, he seems to have disappeared. Again.

[*We see a flicker of a smile from* **Mrs Malone**]

Mrs Malone: I know where he'll be. It should have been our youngest son's birthday today.

10   Cemetery

We see the words on **Snowy's** *gravestone.* **George**, *in pyjama bottoms, slippers and donkey jacket, arrives at the headstone. He takes his cap off. Apart from* **George's** *hard breathing, as if he has just arrived after a long and tiring walk, there is silence. Then he laughs.*

George: Ah son . . . son. It should be you stood here, talking to me . . . like a daft get. [*Another pause. Silence*] Oh son. Son, son, son. I never thought this would happen . . . but here I am, and I'd come every day. If I could. When you love your kids, you love them more than anything else in the whole wide friggin' world, and that's a fact. [*Pause. He talks with anger*] Oh Michael, I miss you son, I'd have willingly taken your place . . . I loved you . . . but if there's anything I can be glad about, we can be glad about, it's that we both knew it, son . . . [*There is a long pause*] Anyway Michael . . . Anyway. [*He tries to laugh*] Oh Christ . . . I feel like James Stewart in 'Shenandoah'.

[*He stays still, his head resting on the headstone. We move back and away from him as he faces out. And we see an ambulance pulling up outside the graveyard*]

11   George's house

The ambulance drives along the road and stops outside the house. We see people at the windows of several houses and watching from doorways. **Mrs Malone** *comes out on the pavement to welcome* **George** *who is returning home.*

Mrs Malone: Hello love, hello pet. Welcome home.

[One of the ambulancemen accompanying **George** *has a small suitcase, the other offers to help him down from the back of the ambulance, but* **George** *protests and rejects the offer and that of a wheelchair. He walks out of the back of the ambulance. The ambulanceman takes the folded up wheelchair and they approach the house.* **Mrs Malone** *takes him inside, helped by the ambulancemen]*

12   George's living room

Mrs Malone *hangs up* **George's** *coat in the hall and enters the living room. The furniture is old-fashioned, traditional, with a definite sense of style and taste. There is also a coal fire blazing away. A huge bookcase lined with books dominates the room. Even more books are stacked up on the floor, at both sides of and in front of the bookcase.* **George** *is seated on a chair with a footstool in front of it. He has several letters in his hand. Some official-looking ones, others obviously 'get well' cards. He opens the official ones first, as he talks.* **Mrs Malone** *goes to the table by the window to arrange the flowers, nodding as she listens.*

George: This is the stuff to give the troops. By god how I looked forward to this.

[She looks at him quizzically and fetches a vase from the fireplace. He looks up]

George: Sitting here by my own fireside. With a clear head, and you. [*He winks at her*]

Mrs Malone: While you fight the good fight.

[*She crosses back to the table*]

George: Well, among other things. But it keeps me occupied. [*He looks up from the letters*] Hm, solicitor's letter. The landlord's solicitor.

Mrs Malone: Old Mr Farrell's house?

George: Listen to this. Execution of termination of tenancy. Eviction order. That's great isn't it. [*With irony, lightly*] Congratulations on reaching the ripe old age of seventy-nine, be out of the house within the month.[*He looks down at the letter*] They want to know who I am, and what business it is of mine. They'll soon find out. [*He drops the letter down*] Bastard landlords . . . and solicitors.

Mrs Malone: You can't do too much, George. Hardly anything. For a while.

George: Look, I can have a go. I'm not going to sit here and do crossword puzzles and stare at the four walls. [*He opens another letter*] Ask Frank Farrell to come round will you please love, in the mornin' sometime.

Mrs Malone: [*Controlling herself, just*] Look, George, I'm not going to stop you doing all this, but —

George: Have you ever?

Mrs Malone: But I am going to tell you when you've had enough.

George: I'll know that myself, love. [*He glances down at the letter*]

Mrs Malone: But that's the trouble — you won't.

[**George** *coughs. Pause*]

Mrs Malone: You won't be able to help anyone if you get to the point where you can't help yourself.

George: Take it easy.

Mrs Malone: Oh aye.

[*He looks at the letter*]

George: Young Katie, eh?

Mrs Malone: Chrissie's sister.

George: Yeah, she's got an appeals tribunal Wednesday week, she'll want representing. I wonder if I ... [*He is already looking at his diary*]

Mrs Malone: Be told will you, you can't go.

[*He holds his hands up in defeat*]

George: OK, OK.

[*She looks disdainful and walks to the door*]

Mrs Malone: John and Ritchie are coming over later.

George: Are the kids coming?

Mrs Malone: Yes.

George: Great. While you're there love, fetch me that good pen of mine and that pad with the lines on.

[*She stares at him as he goes back to studying the letter*]

George: Aye.

[*She goes out*]

13   Living room

We see **George's** *remaining two sons,* **Ritchie** *and* **John**, *who are in their mid and late thirties, informally dressed, sitting at the table with* **George** *and his wife. They are just finishing a meal. But* **George** *has had soup only, and has taken his time with it. On the couch, the three* **grandchildren** *are busy* *demolishing bowls of strawberrry jelly.* **George** *struggles at times for a breath and energy as he talks.* **Ritchie** *quietens the* **kids**.

George: But that's what I'm telling you, that's why you've got to take them out, Ritchie. I mean, you know me, I was never one for taking men out if there was an option, especially if you had to take them back disillusioned and empty-handed.

Ritchie: You know the score, dad.

George: But men can't work under those conditions.

Ritchie: I know, dad. But look, times are hard now, let's face it. And most of them don't want to come out because they're thinking of their few bob.

George: Money before safety.

John: That's the way it is.

John: It's different now, dad. These days, y' go out on strike —

Ritchie: Whatever the reasons —

John: . . . before y' can get out of the gates, management are havin' sing songs an' wearing party hats.

Ritchie: [*Indicating*] With 'Goodbye Boys' written on the front.

John: Come back next week to get your cards.

George: But what are the men thinking about? Y' not goin' to tell me that they're safeguardin' their future — 'cos they've got none whatever way it goes — so they may as well do what's right an' honest.

[*He coughs,* **Anna** *looks up*]

Ritchie: [*Holding his hands up*] Look dad, I stood there yesterday, right John . . .

John: Yeah.

Ritchie: . . . said to them I said, look — this workshop is a deathtrap, one of youse is going to get killed and it won't be a finger or a thumb next time, it'll be two hundredweight of bloody mincemeat lyin' there. They just looked at me.

John: They just stood there, lookin' around, wonderin' who they'd like it to be.

Ritchie: On the floor.

John: As long as it wasn't them.

Ritchie: I tell y', dad, honest to God — I look around sometimes at some of the fellers I'm supposed to be fightin' for . . . they don't seem to care or understand about anythin' that hasn't got tits or comes out of a barrel. I mean that.

George: No, no, no. You're wrong!

Ritchie: I mean it.

Mrs Malone: [*Flaring — starts clearing the table*] And I won't have that kind of defeatist talk at my table. Go and eat jelly with the bairns, go on. And on your way to work in the morning, buy the *Daily Mail*.

John: Ah come on mam, we were just —

Mrs Malone: Talking soft — that's what you were doing, having had it soft most of your lives.

[*The* **brothers** *exchange glances*]

Mrs Malone: Talk to me about hardship and want. Talk to me about no shoes on your feet. Have you any idea what no shoes on your feet means?

John: It means getting y' feet wet when it rains.

Ritchie: And your socks go mouldy.

John: It means the thirties mam, and soup kitchens and hunger marches. You with your father marchin' from the North East, and my dad with his. It means people standing together and fighting. And it means another time and age.

Mrs Malone: And the only reason things got better was because of men like your father, who refused to be slave labour and cannon fodder, who said 'No, I won't go down the docks every morning and stand in a stinking pen, and no I won't beg for half a day's work and come crawling home defeated.'

[*She leaves the table and goes into the kitchen. She continues her speech when she comes back in*]

Mrs Malone: And what's it got better for? So the likes of you can sit back and say you can't do nothing and let it all happen to us again?

[*She storms out of the room, having cleared the contents of the table, except for* **George's** *soup bowl*]

John: What did you let her read Karl Marx for, dad?

George: Dickens.

Ritchie: Pardon?

George: Tale of Two Cities. We are the most important part of the nation. We are the ones who do the work.

[*He coughs heavily. Pause. John's daughter,* **Anna**, *a girl of seven, approaches. She looks at* **George** *carefully*]

George: What can I do for you Anna babe?

Anna: Are you really going to die, grandad?

[*A brief gob-smacked silence. They all look at each other fast, then away*]

George: It has been known to happen.

Anna: What's it like?

John: Enough, enough. Sssshh, sshssshhssshh,

George: Nobody knows, kidder. It's like ... the next episode of ... Spiderman. Nobody knows what it's like ... until it happens.

Anna: I don't like Spiderman.

George: Neither do I.

[*He hugs her, she goes*]

Ritchie: Come on kids. Who wants more jelly?

[*They cheer. We hear* **John's** *voice*]

John: Come on, Anna. Back to the jelly, love.

[*They all go into the kitchen.* **George** *stares out.* **Mrs Malone** *walks back in. He pushes the bowl of soup away. He hasn't touched it. She takes the bowl*]

George: Lovely soup that ...

[**George** *looks at her then away.* **Mrs Malone** *shakes her head and walks to the kitchen*]

14   George's bedroom

The room is functional and old-fashioned, with nothing new, plastic or expensive. The light from a lamp-post struggles through the window and the curtains. In their big double bed, **Mrs Malone** *is lying awake, staring out.* **George** *is asleep, his breathing difficult but regular. Suddenly his body jerks slightly, he groans, and appears to stop breathing for a fraction.* **Mrs Malone** *throws herself across him. And wakes him up.*

Mrs Malone: George!

George: What? [*He turns over and goes to sleep again*]

Mrs Malone: Nothing. It's ... all right. [*She scratches her hands nervously and studies the ceiling*]

15   George's living room

We see the coal fire. We see **Yosser** *sitting down and facing out. He is dressed in clean clothes, is washed and shaved with his hair brushed back, almost too maniacally, away from his face. He is wearing a grey scarf around his neck.*

Yosser: Me mother took me in. In the end ... me mother.

[*Silence. We see* **George** *again. There is a cup and saucer at his side. He looks far from well. He takes his glasses off*]

George: I'm sorry, Yosser, I know you've got your problems, but come to the point, son.

Yosser: I'm better now, George. I reached bottom but ... I'm better now. Better than I was. I'm getting better all the time ... [*He leans forward confidently*] I can see things.

George: What can you see?

Yosser: ... How do you mean? [*Pause*] I want my children back. That's what I want.

George: Go to the social services and talk quietly, behave properly, get the case re-opened, claim custody of the kids, explain your position. Your ma's a good woman. Show them where you live and how you're living.

[**Yosser** *looks away*]

Yosser: I haven't got a chance then.

George: Look Yosser, I know you ... love your kids but you can't inflict your bitterness and hurt on them. Or anyone else, for that matter. Once you've broken something you can't break it again. You've just got to start picking up the pieces.

[**Yosser** *nods*]

Yosser: Why do you know everything?

[**George** *laughs but it turns to coughing.* **Yosser** *gets up, crosses to where* **George** *is sitting and picks him up*]

George: Put me down, you big soft sod! [**Yosser** *puts him down*] I don't know everything. I hardly know bugger all. I just try and apply the little bit I know, and what I learn. To some useful purpose. That's all.

Yosser: I want to be like that. I want to be someone . . . just that. [*He looks down*]

George: Be yourself, Yosser, that's all, just be yourself.

[**Yosser** *looks up.* **George** *is obviously in pain.* **Yosser** *crosses to the door*]

Yosser: But what happens if you don't like yourself?

[**Yosser** *goes out*]

16   George's back living room

Yosser *comes to the doorway and opens the door to reveal* **George'**s *waiting room, in the back living room of the house. Seated are the old man, Frank Farrell, a middle-aged lady, a man in his thirties, and a young woman, drinking tea silently like any waiting room with a tea machine.*

Yosser: Next. [*He laughs*] Next please!

[*Suddenly there is a sound of the cup and saucer smashing in the living room, followed by a quiet thud.* **Yosser** *turns and goes back into the hallway towards the front living room.* **Yosser** *calls 'Mary! Mary!' Frank Farrell follows him. We see* **Mrs Malone** *in the kitchen at the sink, washing potatoes. She turns*]

17   George's bedroom

George *is in bed, asleep.* **Mrs Malone**, *both her* **sons** *and a* **doctor** *are standing by the bed. The* **doctor** *closes his bag.*

Doctor: [*His tone is soft*] I'll pop back before evening surgery. See how he is. All right?

[*The* **doctor** *goes out with* **John**. *Silence*]

Ritchie: That's it, mam, y' know. He can't see anyone else. [*We see* **George** *asleep*] No one else's bastard problems. He's got enough of his own. And I'll stand by that front door and stop them if need be.

[*She silently agrees.* **Ritchie** *crosses over to* **Mrs Malone** *and puts his hands on her shoulders*]

Ritchie: Oh mam.

[**Ritchie** *glances out of the window.* **Chrissie** *and* **Loggo** *are just arriving as the* **doctor** *is leaving*]

Ritchie: It's Chrissie and Loggo.

[*He goes.* **Chrissie** *talks to the* **doctor** *outside. We stay in the room with* **Mrs Malone** *and* **George**. *She goes and sits on the bed. As* **George** *wakes up and looks up at his wife, she takes his hand*]

George: Oh Mary, Mary. What am I doing to you? I'm sorry, girl. I'm in terrible pain, ... it's me stomach, it's just ... it's gone. And the worst thing .. I'm so helpless.

[**Mrs Malone** *looks at him*]

George: I can't, I've got ... no energy. What am I doing to you?

[*She wipes his face with her hand and looks away*]

18   George's house; Saturday, midday

We see **Chrissie** *closing the front door.* **George** *is in the wheelchair outside the door.*

Chrissie: I'll see you, Mary.

[**Chrissie** *starts pushing* **George** *towards the side of the road and the dead docks of the south side.* **George** *is unable to raise his voice, and when he does become enthusiastic he pays heavily for it*]

Chrissie: All right, ace.

George: What a great day, Chrissie.

Chrissie: Where are we going?

George: What about the Baltic? Can you get there, do you think?

Chrissie: Yeah, well, we're going there anyway.

[*They go down the street seen through the railings. The docks are deserted*]

George: I wouldn't have believed it, you know, Chrissie. Look at it.

Chrissie: . . . Look at what?

George: Saturday dinnertime. Not a soul about. Once upon a time, Chrissie . . . once upon a time . . .

Chrissie: If you're going to tell me about Cinderella, I'm taking you home now.

[*We see them walk along the pavement above the dead docks. Each phase of* **George's** *speech is shot in a different area of wasteland and indiscriminate destruction until we reach their destination*]

19   Dock area

George *is being pushed by* **Chrissie** *along the bridge leading to the dead docks.*

George: Saturday afternoon. We'd have been looking forward to it from the previous Saturday — payday Saturday you know — no five-day week and off to the Leisure Centre then, boyo. Ah, there'd be hundreds of us coming along here, the ship repair men, scalers, dockers, the Mary Ellens who used to swab the big liners, and behind us the great big Shire cart horses.

[They walk through a huge scrapyard full of rusty metal]

George: Ah Chrissie, and there were many a good old horse who walked down the hill with us who came back up in the knackers' carts. The vet'd put a gun to his head and a straw bolster around its neck, and wind it up into the knacker's cart, and its big head turning. You could still see the whites of its eye ... and yet the horses of privilege that pose outside Buckingham Palace and ponce and parade up and down the Mall were turned out into a meadow of cowslip and clover and guaranteed a full proven bag for the rest of their lives.

[They reach the waterfront along the River Mersey]

George: Ah Chrissie, it just seems like soddin' yesterday, the midday gun. The women sandstoning the steps and the flags. The kids playing alley-oh, the little shops on the corner where you got the three pennyworth of fine Irish, the old snuff, and the twist of tobacco, and your old gran had a flat top cart there, used to sell salt fish and a big barrel of ribs, straight off the pig's back from the Irish boats and on the third Saturday an organ grinder and his monkey ...

20   Docks

They continue along the waterfront.

George: And there we'd be pilin' into Effin' Nellie's or Peg-
leg Pete's, for a couple of pints of good beer, maybe the
first in the week and the crack . . . the crack . . . we'd talk of
many things . . .

[*We hear* **Chrissie's** *voice*]

Chrissie: Of cabbages and Kings.

[*They walk through a derelict warehouse in the Albert Docks
and look up at the rafters*]

George: Of politics and power and come the day when we'd
have inside toilets and proper bathrooms. Of Attlee and
Bevan, Hogan and Logan, the Braddocks and Dixie Dean
. . . and Lawton and Liddell and Matthews and Finney . . .
of Come the Revolution and the Blackpool Illuminations
. . . Joseph Jones had a violin, a 'Stradavarious', he
said . . .

21   Container base

We see **George** *and* **Chrissie** *going silently through a
container base on the Dock Road, past row upon row of
containers, being dwarfed by them. A stacker-truck passes
them by. A flock of birds takes off in front of them.*

22   The Albert Docks

George *and* **Chrissie** *are now in the same setting as in Scene
4, surrounded by beautiful, derelict ruins.* **George** *is sitting in
the wheelchair;* **Chrissie** *is pushing him.*

George: Well we've got our bathrooms . . . At considerable expense . . . I write letters to prison for the mother of a man who rapes little boys, but there's hundreds of friggin' rapists still running free.

[**George** *waves to* **Chrissie** *to stop. They do*]

George: Get me up, son. Get me up, Chrissie.

Chrissie: Are you sure, George?

George: Yeah.

[**Chrissie** *comes around to the front of the wheelchair. He lifts* **George** *up, gently, then holds him in his arms and hugs him. Long and hard. When he releases* **George***,* **George** *just looks at him and nods once. He doesn't need to ask.* **Chrissie** *stands him up against the wall and holds him there*]

George: Forty-seven years ago, I stood here, a young bull, and watched my first ship come in . . . They say that memories live longer than dreams . . . But my dreams, those dreams, those dreams of long ago, they still give me some kind of hope and faith in my class . . . I can't believe there is no hope, I can't.

[*He just stares out*]

Chrissie: Hey, come on, George, your lads'll be in the Baltic Fleet now, you know. Pints on the bar . . . Loggo said he might come over . . .

[*We see* **Chrissie** *getting* **George** *back in the wheelchair*]

Chrissie: Christ, George, you're getting heavy.

[**Chrissie** *puts* **George's** *feet on the footrest.* **Chrissie** *is on his haunches looking at* **George**]

Chrissie: George . . .

[**George** *is completely still.* **Chrissie** *reaches to touch his face, almost to feel his breath, but doesn't*]

Chrissie: They'll be waiting for us you know, George.

[**Chrissie** *looks round over his shoulder*]

Chrissie: Oh Jesus.

[**Chrissie** *then suddenly stands up, turns and runs. First one way, then the other. And runs. And runs. From a distance, we see* **George** *in the wheelchair and* **Chrissie** *running along the derelict dockside. Slow fade to black*]

23   George's bedroom

Pan up from black to see **Mrs Malone** *with* **George**'s *body in a coffin on a stand. The coffin, which hasn't yet been closed, is barely seen in the shadows.* **Mrs Malone** *is sitting still and erect on a hard-backed chair facing the bed.*

24   George's bedroom

Daylight comes in through the drawn curtains onto the candle, crucifix and madonna on the table. Then a knock at the bedroom door. The door opens. **Ritchie** *comes in.*

Ritchie: . . . They're here, Mam.

[*She nods*]

25   George's living room

The room, which is wildly overcrowded, is full of people looking at the carpet. We see **Mrs Malone** *go by the doorway with* **Ritchie**. **John** *comes into the room.*

John: ... First car.

[*As the mourners troop out of the living room, we see* **Chrissie** *and* **Loggo** *in there at the back. They look through the curtains then walk out. We see sitting alone on a couch, hidden until now,* **George's** *grand-daughter,* **Anna.** *She is eating a packet of crisps as tears silently trip her. She keeps eating through the tears*]

26 George's house

The curtains are drawn in every house in the street. People line the streets, some still coming out of the houses. We see the funeral cars, and a line of cars behind them. The procession of cars sets off down the road. **Yosser** *is standing silently in the road, apart from the crowd. Head down he starts walking with the procession. We see* **Ritchie, John** *and* **Mrs Malone** *in the first car as it follows the hearse. We see old men taking their caps off, women blessing themselves, people waving strange little waves, like children. As the car carrying* **George** *goes past them, an old lady stumbles towards the car, crying* 'God rest you son, God be with you,' *and is led away.* **Mrs Malone** *is upset and calmed by* **Ritchie** *and* **John.**

Mrs Malone: Bless her.

Ritchie and John: It's all right, Mum.

27 The church

We see three altar boys walk down the aisle to the altar. The younger two are chatting and are told to 'be quiet' by the older one. They place the candles on the altar table and the crucifix against the wall. They stand by the wall. **John, Ritchie** *and* **Chrissie** *and three older men carry the coffin down the aisle towards the altar, followed by the close mourners. The* *congregation is standing, filling the pews. The* **priest** *is walking ahead of the coffin.*

Priest: Show your mercy, Lord, to this departed servant of yours. Since he strove to do your will, let him not be punished for wrongdoing. And as he was united in the true faith with all your faithful people, let him now by your loving goodness be united with the angelic throng. Through Christ our Lord. I know that my Redeemer lives, and that on the last day I shall rise again; and in my flesh I shall see God, my Saviour. I myself shall see Him: with my own eyes I shall gaze upon Him: And in my flesh I shall see God, my Saviour. This is the hope which is laid up in my heart: And in my flesh I shall see God, my Saviour.

[*The* **priest** *turns, as the coffin reaches the step to the altar. The funeral attendants take the coffin from the bearers and place it on the trestles. We see* **Dixie** *and* **Kevin** *and* **Loggo** *among the rows of familiar faces. At the back of the church we see* **Yosser** *enter, and stand against the wall. The close mourners file into the pews at the front of the church, and the family sit in the front pew. The congregation are standing.* **Mrs Malone** *and the* **children** *wait. The* **priest** *blows his nose. The coffin is lowered onto the trestles.* **Chrissie** *watches. The funeral attendants bow. The* **priest** *turns and approaches the altar, genuflects, kisses it and starts the service. The altar boys chat briefly then concentrate*]

Priest: In the name of the Father and of the Son and of the Holy Spirit Amen. The Grace of our Lord Jesus Christ and the love of God and the fellowship of the Holy Spirit be with you all.

Congregation: And also with you.

Priest: My brothers and sisters, to prepare ourselves to celebrate the sacred mysteries, let us call to mind our sins.

[*We cut outside to see the three funeral cars outside the church. The drivers are having a smoke, reading newspapers and cleaning the car windows. We come back into the church*]

Priest: Rejoice and be glad for your reward will be great in Heaven, this is how they persecuted the prophets before you. This is the Gospel of the Lord.

Congregation: Praise to you Lord Jesus Christ.

[*Congregation sit automatically*]

Priest: [*To* **Yosser**] Please sit down.

[**Yosser** *just stands in the middle of the aisle. The* **priest** *withers him.* **Yosser** *moves back and sits on the end of a pew making someone move up for him.* **Loggo** *turns round and sees* **Yosser** *sit*]

Priest: My dear friends, may I say that I have never seen so many people gathered here to pay their last respects. I am sure that the family of Patrick Malone must —

[**Ritchie** *stand and interrupts the* **priest**. *He is tight-lipped and angry*]

Ritchie: George Malone. My father's name was George.

Priest: I'm sorry. [*He quickly looks down at his notes just to make sure.* **Ritchie** *sits*] But he was christened here in this very church as Patrick, and that is his name as known to Almighty God.

[**Ritchie** *stands again*]

Ritchie: I don't care what his name was known by under Almighty God. Patrick Malone means nothing to the people here. His name was George Malone. That's how he was known by all of us. George Malone.

[*He sits and suddenly puts his head down. His mother quietly takes his hand, while still staring out*]

Priest: ... I am sure that the family of George Malone must be proud of the recognition and respect accorded to this man. To George Malone. The Acts of the Apostles perhaps best sum up the effect that this one man's life must have had on all who met him. It says in the Acts of the Apostles, 'Silver and gold have I none; but such as I have, give I thee.' From what I have learnt of Pa— George Malone, I believe that this noble and fine sentiment pertains to him.

[*He switches to automatic pilot*]

Of one thing be certain, however, and at this sad time, when by nature of why we are gathered here this morning, we must be aware of our own mortality, let us remember that we are all children of Almighty God, we are all here on this good earth till He calls us to Him, and we must always, in the word of the Lord, 'stand ready, because the Son of Man is coming at an hour you do not expect'. And with this in mind, I would like to remind you of my earlier reading from the Romans, Chapter 14 verses 7 to 12 ...

[*And as the* **priest** *goes on to describe the joys of mortality, death and judgement we see* **Ritchie** *and* **John** *glaring at the* **priest***, getting more and more tense. The other people on the front pew exchange glances, except for* **Mrs Malone***, who bows her head. By the end of the speech,* **Chrissie** *and* **John** *are having to hold* **Ritchie** *down*]

... The life and death of each of us has its influence on others. If we live, we live for the Lord; and if we die, we die for the Lord. This explains why Christ both died and came to life, it was so that he might be Lord both of the dead and the living. This is also why you should never pass judgement on a brother or treat him with contempt. We shall have to stand before the judgement seat of God; as scripture says: Be my life — it is the Lord who speaks — every knee shall bend before me, and every tongue shall praise God. It is to God, therefore, that each of us must give an account of —

[**Chrissie** *stands up and speaks. He hates every second, but he has to say it. As he speaks we also see* **Angie***, his wife, in the pew behind him, tearful, proud and understanding*]

Chrissie: I'm sorry Father, but you're not on. We haven't come here to listen to this. The last thing I want to do is to stand up and interrupt you, but you'd better know — we're all here today not to send George to a better place or a judgement day, or to worry about our own going, but to remember his life and curse the fact that he's not here. He was a good man. He was the best man I ever knew. I . . . I loved George Malone, and our lives are going to be a lot emptier now that he's not here. He didn't do nothing for no rewards. Not here, nor in . . . Heaven.

[**Chrissie** *sits down, head down.* **Ritchie** *puts his hands on* **Chrissie's***. We see the* **priest***. He finally speaks with some semblance of dignity and awareness*]

Priest: Well . . . yes. It would appear that the Church has very little to do here but to pay its own respects to George Malone. And I understand that. I am aware of the intensity. Of feeling. A good life lost has little compensation. To those who remain . . . In the name of the Father and of the Son and of the Holy Ghost.

28 Cemetery

There is a large crowd of mourners. The coffin is in the ground. The **priest** *has said the end of the burial service. The grave-digger gives the family some earth. They throw it into the grave,* *and go.* **Mrs Malone** *is left alone with her grief as people start to move away from the grave.* **Ritchie, John** *and* **Chrissie** *comfort each other. At this point we hear* **Mrs Malone** *fall onto the coffin from the graveside. We see* **Chrissie, Ritchie** *and* **John** *fetch her out, helped by the* **hospital doctor.** *They walk with her and the other mourners to the cars. We see* **Yosser,** *a lone figure on higher ground. He turns and walks away.*

29   George's living room

After the funeral. Ham and tuna and cheese sandwiches are being handed round by old ladies, as well as madeira cake, cups of tea, sherry and whisky. We see children eating, and groups of men clustered in the corners, with the women sitting around, or standing in similar groups. The **priest** *is alone, drinking whisky quickly.* **John** *enters the room. He talks to no one in particular.*

John: No bones broken. She's all right.

[*There is a murmur of relief.* **John** *goes into the front room.* **Loggo** *and* **Chrissie** *stand together.* **Chrissie, Loggo,** *then* **John** *come into the back room. Someone is humming, the* **priest** *is in the background drinking.* **John** *looks over at the* **priest** *who says* 'a decent man, George' *to* **Loggo** *and* **Chrissie. Chrissie** *glances at* **Loggo.** *He indicates out,* **Loggo** *nods, they go. The* **priest** *puts his glass down.* **Loggo** *and* **Chrissie** *go to the front door, but when they open it, they stop. They see* **Yosser,** *across the road on the other pavement, staring at* **George's** *house*]

Loggo: [*Turning away*] Oh frig!
Chrissie: Out the back.

[*They close the door. We see* **Yosser** *closer*]

30   George's back kitchen

They go into the back kitchen to reach the back door. We see
John *and* **Ritchie** *alone as a woman goes past carrying a tray
of tea. Both brothers are sitting sombrely side by side at the
back kitchen table.* 'One of us will have to stay here with her,
that's for sure.' *They see* **Loggo** *and* **Chrissie** *and immediately
stand up.* **Loggo** *ducks towards the back door.*

Loggo: OK, lads. See you again. Look after yourselves.

Ritchie: Thank you lads.

[**Chrissie** *puts his hands up*]

Chrissie: No sweat. Take care of yourselves.

John: Take it easy, boys.

[**Chrissie** *too ducks out as fast as he can before the brothers
can approach and thank him*]

31   Back yard

We see the **priest** *on his knees. He has been sick into a grid. We
see* **Chrissie** *behind.* **Loggo,** *waiting for* **Chrissie,** *loosens his
collar and watches the* **priest**. **Chrissie** *also looks at the*
priest *then moves off.* **Loggo** *nods to* **Chrissie** *and goes into
the alleyway.* **Chrissie** *follows. They walk down the alleyway
from the camera.*

Chrissie: Have we got much on this afternoon?

Loggo: Not a lot.

Chrissie: How much money have we got?

Loggo: Enough.

Chrissie: Good. 'Cos I'm going to get arseholed.

32   Pub

We see the interior of the public bar, and it is not a pretty sight: bedlam alive and well. It is just after midday of a Thursday. There is a pool table and fruit machine on the go. 'Imagine' has been on the jukebox and people are still singing it. A vociferous game of cards is in progress in a barely seen corner. We see 'If I Were a Blackbird' being whistled and sung by **'Ronny Renaldo'***. He is sitting near* **Gnasher Llewellyn** *and his dummy. Every so often he sings and whistles 'If I Were a Blackbird'. We hardly focus on him or* **Gnasher** *until they perform. The television is showing a wild life programme. But the sound has been turned down. We focus briefly on an* **elderly waiter/glass collector***, who is doing his job slightly faster than he should be. He repeats continually* 'Empty your glasses, please' *and when he has collected all the glasses up, he puts them back on the tables and starts again. As the scene develops, the speed at which he operates increases, and at every chance he drinks the dregs from the bottom of each glass, making a yodelling noise as he does so. It is all a madness understated.*

Loggo: That's what I like about this place, Chrissie — it's nice and quiet at lunchtimes.

[**Loggo** *and* **Chrissie** *are at the bar getting their drinks. They grin at each other.* **Loggo** *indicates* **Dixie** *and* **Kevin***, who now come into our view.* **Chrissie** *and* **Loggo** *move down the bar towards them. We also see the* **pub manager** *at the optic, taking pills. In a pop-eyed manner*]

Loggo: All right fellas!

Chrissie: All right lads!

Chrissie: I thought you went away Kev.

Kevin: I did.

Chrissie: What happened?

Kevin: I came back.

[*Silence.* **Kevin** *and* **Dixie** *finish their drinks*]

Loggo: Do you fellas want another or what?

Dixie: Not from you two, no.

[**Dixie** *starts to move away, followed by* **Kevin**]

Chrissie: Ah come on, Dix . . .

[*But* **Dixie** *and* **Kevin** *walk out*]

Loggo: Well you can't win them all.

[*The bar room door opens again. They both look across and then rapidly away and down*]

Loggo: Oh shite, not 'Shake-hands'!

[*We see* '**Shake-hands**', *a big man in his early forties, in trim. When he speaks it is a hoarse whisper like a man with a serious throat disorder or a fixation with Marlon Brando's performance in 'The Godfather'. The* **manager** *pops his pills when he sees* **Shake-hands** *too.* **Shake-hands** *approaches the bar and* **Loggo** *and* **Chrissie**]

Shake-hands: Shake hands.

Loggo: [*Not looking*] I've got dermatitis, Shakes.

Shake-hands: [*Same intonation*] Shake hands.

[**Loggo** *offers him his hand, wincing already.* **Shake-hands** *shakes hands, with both his hands.* **Loggo** *groans with pain*]

Shake-hands: What d' you want?

Loggo: An ambulance [**Shake-hands** *grins broadly*] Pint of bitter, Shakes.

[**Shake-hands** *faces the bar, speaks to absolutely nobody, very quietly, just in case someone is there and hiding*]

Shake-hands: Pint of bitter, boss.

Collector: [*Hurrying past*] Empty y' glasses now please! [*We see him in action*] Come on, ladies, let's have your glasses please.

Loggo: At ten past twelve!

[**Loggo** *blows on his injured hand.* **Shake-hands** *is now out of view, but we can still hear him*]

Shake-hands: Shake hands.

[*The* **manager** *re-appears, quietly twitching, heavily harassed and totally worn out*]

Manager: [*Half-hearted*] Oh come on, Shakes. You're barred out.

Shake-hands: Shake hands.

Manager: But I'll let you off this time. What y' havin'?

Shake-hands: [*Louder*] Pint of bitter please, Joseph, thank you very much.

[*Only* **Shake-hands** *gets a drink. The* **collector** *comes back. We see the* **four youths** *in the corner laughing*]

Collector: Let's have your glasses now, please!

[*As he speaks, he snatches* **Loggo's** *unfinished pint of bitter. As* **Loggo** *goes to pick it up we see the* **collector** *drinking it as he hurries away*]

Loggo: What's up with him?

Manager: Those dick-heads over there slipped some speed into the slops. [*We see the* **youths** *again*] knowin' full well he drinks the dregs. I tried to lock him in the toilet before but he broke the bloody door down.

Shake-hands: That's not nice. I like Harold. He's my friend.

[*Meanwhile, out of view* **Ronny Renaldo** *has once again started whistling and singing 'If I Were a Blackbird I Would Whistle and Sing'. The* **glass collector** *is putting bottles on the youths' table when* **Shake-hands** *walks over, faces the four* **youths** *and challenges them*]

Shake-hands: Shake hands.

[*But we stay with* **Loggo**, **Chrissie** *and the* **manager** *and hear* **Shake-hands** *saying, louder this time, 'Shake hands now!'*]

Manager: [*Sighs*] Has he had a go at yours, as well?

Chrissie: Er — yeah.

[**Chrissie** *and* **Loggo** *exchange knowing glances. Although we can't see* **Shake-hands**, *we can still hear him: 'Shake hands, shake hands now.' Then, still out of view, the* **first youth** *screams. The* **manager** *tops up.* **Chrissie's** *pint*]

Manager: I tell y'. I'll be glad when I'm gone. I've been due a move for nearly nine months but they can't get anyone else to come here.

[*The* **manager** *looks over the the* **youths'** *table as the* **second youth** *screams*]

Manager: I wouldn't mind but —

[*He looks across towards* **Shake-hands**]

Shake-hands: Pint of bitter for the boy.

[*The* **manager** *looks regularly and very quickly at the scene. And at the same time, at every opportunity, he slips a double whisky into the glass he's already got*]

Manager: I wouldn't mind but —

[*Again,* **Shake-hands'** *voice carries from across the room. It is now very loud*]

Shake-hands: Am I talking to myself? Shake hands.

Manager: And if I find out who's bringing the home brew in here . . .

Youth: [*Unseen*] Aaaaah! Get off.

[*The **manager** is now drinking hard and fast*]

Manager: I wouldn't mind, but three years ago —

[*He looks across as we hear screams of pain from the area round **Shake-hands**. He pours himself another whisky as he talks, hesitates and then turns it into a double*]

Manager: Three years ago . . .

Shake-hands: [*Unseen*] Make that two pints. Shake hands.

Manager: . . . three years ago, this was a quiet pub. There was only . . . there was only fights at the weekends and weddings.

[*Out of sight, the **third youth** gives a groan of pain*]

Manager: I mean if they go . . .

[*The **manager** looks over to the lads, then double-takes. We see **Shake-hands** with the **third youth** who slumps to the floor*]

Shake-hands: Make that three pints, boss.

Manager: . . . if they got legless they danced on the tables. Now they break them over each others' heads. Someone is bringing home-brew in here y' know. I know they are.

[*The **glass collector** approaches*]

Collector: Empty your glasses please.

[**Loggo** *and* **Chrissie** *close up to protect their glasses. The* **collector** *tries to grab them but is repulsed*]

Manager: They've all got too much time to kill, that's what it is.

*[We see **Shake-hands** pursuing a **fourth lad** who hides under the table]*

Shake-hands: Shake hands. Am I talking to myself?

Fourth youth: Get lost, will you!

Shake-hands: Shake hands.

Fourth youth: Pick on someone your own size.

*[**Shake-hands** turns the table over and chases the **youth** to the window. We hear him say 'Shake hands' as, yet again, **Ronny Renaldo** bursts into song]*

Manager: Let's face facts, boys, it's bedlam in here. Just look at them, just friggin' look at them.

*[**Shake-hands** pulls the **fourth youth** off the window ledge onto the floor. There are shouts of 'Leave the kid alone!' As the **youth** cries 'Oh me bum!']*

Manager: Just take a look around — we all had something to give. I mean Gnasher, over there, Gnasher *[Over **Ronny's** whistling]* He never gnashed until Tate and Lyle laid him off. And Ronny over there was a waiter at the Adelphi. The last thing he did was rob the uniform when he left, had no time for his friggin' whistlin' — then.

*[The **manager** takes money for the next pint from **Loggo**, walks towards the till, stops, and pockets the money. He turns back]*

Manager: Shake-hands — he was a bouncer in town. At least two of those kids had apprenticeships. Everyone was either respectable or a villain.

Collector: *[Out of view]* Hurry along there please. Haven't you got homes to go to? *[He makes a noise like a train]*

[*The **manager** has another drink then continues his speech*]

Manager: They had good reason to get pissed. Now they just get pissed 'cos they wish they were dead.

[*Another drink*]

Manager: And so do I.

[*He looks across at the mayhem and helps himself to more whisky*]

Manager: After all, this is only buildin' up for Saturday night.

[*Suddenly, the **redundancy party** arrives: six big redundant men enter the pub*]

First man: [*Already half-cut*] Set them up, Joe! This is going to be a night to end all nights!

[*The **manager** heads for the whisky*]

Manager: Oh shite, not another redundancy party.

[*He crosses to the optic, then looks round*]

First man: Listen, Joey. Come here, mate, I want four bitters . . .

Manager: Every single one barred out already. What am I going to do?

[*The **manager** does the whisky into a treble. The **men** are at the bar. The **first man** is shouting his order still*]

Manager: [*To himself*] The manager of the Eagle's got a shotgun . . . [*Then he turns to **Chrissie** and **Loggo**] I'd only shoot myself if I had one. [*He turns to the **redundancy part**] What?

First man: Listen Joey, come on listen, come on! I want four bitters, a golden and a lager, plus five whiskys and a gin an' tonic for the puff.

Second man: [*Six-foot-nine and seventeen stone*] Leave off, bollocks . . .

First man: [*Putting a roll of money on the counter*] There y' are, Joey. When that's gone, let us know. What do you want, fellas?

[*The* **manager** *takes the money*]

Chrissie: [*Watching it all*] Time to go, Loggo.

Loggo: Hang on, Chrissie, let me finish my pint.

First man: [*Turning to the room*] What d' y' want fellers? Anything y' want.

Loggo: No you're all right, Mick, we're sound.

First man: Come 'head, Loggo, what's up with y' — y' look as though y've been to a funeral.

[**Loggo** *and* **Chrissie** *look at each other.* **Chrissie** *raises his eyebrows slightly*]

First man: Look boys. I've got a grand here. Once it's gone, it's gone, frig it.

Loggo: No y' all right, Mick we're in.

First man: Y' can be in again, can't y'. Two more pints over here, Joey.

[*He goes. Now* **Shake-hands** *is approaching the bar, flexing his fingers*]

Shake-hands: Large brandy, Michael. Much appreciated.

First man: I won't ask you again. What d' y' all want?

[*We see* **Ronny Renaldo** *walk across to the bar and sit, still singing and whistling*]

Ronny Renaldo: If I were a blackbird I would whistle and sing.

First man: He wants brain surgery.

[*But the* **second man** *hugs* **Ronny**]

Second man: It was a lousy job anyway. [*He goes back to the bar as the* **glass collector** *arrives*]

Collector: Hurry along now ladies . . .

First man: [*To* **Gnasher**] What do you want, eh?

Gnasher: [*Between gnashes*] Whisky and dry ginger please.

First man: [*Gnashing back*] It's my pleasure. [*He mimics him*] Whisky and dry ginger please.

[*The barmaids are busy serving*]

Chrissie: I'm goin' now. You have mine.

Loggo: Hang on, I'll just . . .

[*The* **glass collector** *takes* **Loggo's** *pint out of his hand*]

Loggo: . . . come with you.

[**Ronny Renaldo** *is at the bar whistling, surrounded by drinkers. We see the whole pub, noisy and chaotic. We hear the* **first man**, 'Four more pints over here, Joey, for the playschool outing'. **Ronny** *is still whistling*]

First man: Shut up Ronny, will y', y' getting on me tits.

[*The* **manager** *puts his head in his hands*]

First man: Where's my bevvy, then eh?

[*He grabs* **Loggo's** *arm as he and* **Chrissie** *go by*]

First man: Hey Loggo, you're not off are y'?

Loggo: I've got to get out of this friggin' asylum.

First man: Have another one. Two more pints.

[*The* **glass collector** *takes his pint. He turns back*]

First man: Hey, where's my soddin' drink then? Hey, come back here.

[*Camera pans with* **Chrissie** *and* **Loggo***. And then* **Yosser** *walks into the bar, looking dangerous and vacant.* **Chrissie** *and* **Loggo** *see* **Yosser**]

Loggo: Oh frig!

[**Yosser** *stands in the middle of the bar.* **Shake-hands** *walks up to him*]

Shake-hands: Shake hands.

[*They are left alone together. The* **manager** *looks on horrified.* **Yosser** *stares at* **Shake-hands***, and then down at* **Shake-hands'** *hands*]

Shake-hands: Shake hands. Shake hands.

[**Shake-hands** *takes hold of* **Yosser's** *hand with both his hands and begins shaking it. Hardly any movement, not big at all.* **Yosser** *seems to stare curiously at* **Shake-hands***. Then looks down at the hands gripping him, then back at* **Shake-hands'** *face. And as they stand close together staring at each other,* **Yosser** *butts him.* **Shake-hands** *reacts with a grin as his nose bursts, then goes to fall back and down. However, as he still has hold of* **Yosser's** *hand with both of his hands, he stays at sixty degrees for a second or so*]

Ronny Renaldo: If I were a blackbird I would whistle and sing.

[*Then* **Yosser** *releases his grip.* **Shake-hands** *falls flat on his back.* **Yosser** *looks at him*]

Shake-hands: Another pint of bitter, boss. [*And out*]

[*The pub crowd laugh.* **Yosser** *looks around and shrugs almost in apology and regret*]

33 Outside the pub

Chrissie *and* **Loggo** *leave the pub. But still we can hear* **Ronny Renaldo** *whistling.* **Loggo** *lights a cigarette.* **Chrissie** *joins him and they lean against the wall.*

Chrissie: George is dead.

Loggo: So y've said.

Chrissie: Yeah. But George is dead.

Loggo: I know, Chrissie, *I know.*

Chrissie: But . . . you know what he stood for, don't y'?

Loggo: What do you mean?

[**Chrissie** *shakes his head*]

Chrissie: Yeah. Well that's dead an' all isn't it?

[*As* **Chrissie** *finishes speaking and they begin to walk away, we hear a chorus echoing from the pub.* 'For Christ's sake, Ronny, I told you to shut up. All right Ronny you're gonna go.' **Chrissie** *and* **Loggo** *stop and listen*]

Choir: A one . . . two . . . a three!

[*And flying through the pub window comes* **Ronny Renaldo***, still holding onto his chair, and then landing on the pavement while still sitting on his chair, unscathed. He sits facing the roadway. He begins singing, cheerfully*]

Ronny Renaldo: 'Well I never felt more like singing the blues, 'cos I never thought I'd ever lose your love, dear, you got me singin' the blues . . . I never felt more like cryin' all night.' etc

[*We see the* **pub manager** *walking out of the same exit. He is putting his coat on, as he goes. But he still has the large glass of whisky. He approaches* **Chrissie** *and* **Loggo**]

Pub manager: It's either them or me — and it's them.

[*The* **manager** *goes out of our vision, across the road. We hear a sharp squeal of brakes and the sound of a glass smashing, and a car driver shouting abuse.* 'Hey, you dickhead! Are you blind?']

[*The* **manager** *stumbles on to the opposite side of the road and walks away*]

Chrissie: There isn't a soul in there who is certified. They are all sane people.

[*There is a pause*]

Chrissie: What is going wrong, Loggo? What is going wrong?

Loggo: Everything, lah, everything.

[*They stay there as* **Yosser** *comes out of the entrance they came out of. He approaches them, but stays a few yards away. He stares out in the manner that they are staring out. They glance at him and look away.* **Chrissie** *glances up at the sky*]

Chrissie: Beam me up, Scotty. Beam me up.

[**Loggo** *looks up too.* **Yosser** *looks at them, then looks up. We see their point of view — a derelict, part-demolished warehouse,* 'Tate & Lyle's 1922', *written across the front.* **Yosser** *turns to them and stares closely at them, then up again, then to them*]

Yosser: . . . Gizza job, go on, gizza job.

[**Chrissie** *and* **Loggo** *look at each other and visibly slump their shoulders. They turn and walk away, leaving* **Yosser***. We see the warehouse being demolished, then we see the three of them walking along,* **Yosser** *following a few yards behind them, shambling along. He digs in a dustbin and finds a plastic bag. We finally see them walking along the road and into the sunset*]

[*Freeze frame*]

Follow-up Activities

Discussion

Jobs for the Boys

1 Is it possible to divide the characters in this play into 'heroes' and 'villains'? Which, if any, deserve each label?

2. In what ways is the fact that it is Snowy who is killed particularly moving or poignant?

3 What examples of 'black' comedy can you find in this play?

Moonlighter

1 Do you believe moonlighting is morally wrong? Both employed and unemployed people go moonlighting. Is it more (or less) immoral in either case?

2 What is Dixie's attitude to moonlighting? What pressures drive him to it?

3 Do you expect to have to leave your home town in order to find a job? Will you be prepared to do so?

Shop Thy Neighbour

1 What is the relationship between Chrissie and Angie at the end of this play?

2 Philip Saville, the director of *Boys from the Blackstuff*, asked Alan Bleasdale to rewrite the original third script

to include a woman's point of view: 'Go away and write Angie!' Do you find Angie a convincing and/or sympathetic character?

Yosser's Story

1 Why do you think it was Yosser who especially caught the imagination of the public when the series was first shown?
2 Besides the literal sense, in what ways is Yosser 'hitting his head against a brick wall'?
3 Some critics have described this play as being less realistic and more 'surrealist' than the others. Why should this be? Do you agree with this view?

George's Last Ride

1 Why is George such a respected and liked member of his community?
2 Just before his death, he says he has some kind of hope and faith in his class. What does he mean? Is he justified?
3 What would be your answer to Chrissie when he says (Scene 33) that what George stood for is dead?

General points

(Each of these may be relevantly discussed after reading any of the scripts.)

1 What impact do the plays have on you? What emotions do they arouse?
2 Which are your favourite scenes? Why?
3 Which characters do you find particularly credible or sympathetic?
4 Which characters are politically militant or active? What happens to each of them?
5 Do you think the DoE characters are presented as 'villains'?

6 'Every time a genuinely heartless official appeared, it was a woman ... On the other hand, the men's parts were nearly always softened.' That criticism of the series was made by Ruth Smith in an article called 'A Feminist View', published in *The Leveller* (February 1983). What evidence can you find to support or contradict her view? Do you feel it is fair comment?

7 Alan Bleasdale has said he does not find it easy to write women's roles. Are the female characters, as Ruth Smith (see above) has suggested, all stereotypes? Or do you feel the plays present a realistic portrayal of women in such a society?

8 Do you think the comedy undermines or re-inforces the serious points the plays are making?

9 'Life in Liverpool is a tragedy played as a comedy.' In which ways is this Merseyside 'proverb' true of *Boys from the Blackstuff*?

10 Do you feel that, in any way, the plays paint too bleak a view of the situation?

11 Do you think the series is basically optimistic or pessimistic?

12 Alan Bleasdale has said on a radio programme: 'I don't think I'm a political writer. Other people do.' Do you think he is a political writer? Do you think the plays are a form of propaganda?

13 How do you think the stories and characters might have differed (if at all) if the plays had been set in another city?

14 Many comfortably-off, employed, middle-class viewers and critics praised the series. Why do you think this was so?

15 Do you believe that a play (or a poem or novel or film) can change society in any way?

Work and unemployment

1 What do we mean by 'work'? Is it paid activity? Activity with a purpose? (For example, is looking after a vegetable garden 'work' or a hobby? What about looking after a flower garden?)

2 Is work desirable? A necessary evil? Essential? Is it 'a good thing'? Would you like not to have to work? Would you like not to have a job?

3 What are the practical and emotional problems of being unemployed? For a married person? A single person? A school leaver?

4 How does society view the unemployed? Have attitudes changed over recent years?

5 What do you think will be the job situation when your children are leaving school?

6 Are more benefits and allowances the answers to unemployment?

7 How can people without jobs be helped to feel useful and to keep their dignity?

8 How can people be helped to use 'free' time more satisfyingly?

Writing

1 Choose one of the plays and write two reviews of it, each of about 300 words, which might have appeared in extreme right-wing and extreme left-wing newspapers.

2 Select one of the minor characters (e.g., a social worker) from *Boys from the Blackstuff* and write a short story with him or her as the central character.

3 Express your own thoughts, prompted by one of the plays or characters, in the form of a poem or song lyrics.

4 Imagine you write an 'agony' column in a magazine. A young person has written a letter to your column complaining about boredom and lack of spending money when unemployed, and asking how he or she can fill his or

her spare time. Write an answer for publication.

5   Write short entries for an encyclopedia explaining the words (or concepts) 'job' and 'work'.

Other projects

1   From your local Health and Social Security and Unemployment Benefit offices or Advice Bureaux, find out to what benefits an unemployed person is at present entitled (e.g., Supplementary, Unemployment, Maternity, etc.). Where and how can such benefits be obtained? How much time can you spend in part-time education and how much can you earn from part-time work without losing these benefits?

2   Improvise a series of scenes on the theme of getting (or not getting) a job. Limit the number of characters, but include family scenes, scenes at a Jobcentre, at the Department of Health and Social Security, places of work, etc. Develop (and perhaps script) them into a play.

3   Plan how a group of unemployed young people might try to set up a business of their own. How should they decide on what kind of business? What would be the advantages of 'going it alone'? What problems would they face? What mistakes might they make? How could they lower the risks? What advice would you give them? Information is available from the Small Firms Information Service (Freefone 2444).

4   Choose an issue about which you feel strongly. Hold a debate on that topic with the motion, 'It isn't fair that . . .'.

5   Invent a character who is a victim of the situation you have debated. Improvise a short play about that character. Develop your improvisation into a stage or television script. Remember that some scenes in a television play may be just images, some just dialogue

and others a mixture of dialogue and action. Try to hear in your mind how your characters speak as you write your lines.

In groups, rehearse your scripts and then discuss and revise them so that they are both more convincing and more telling.

STUDIO SCRIPTS

Series editor: David Self

Working
The Boy with the Transistor Radio   *Willy Russell*
Good Prospects   *Charlie Stafford*
Strike   *Yolanda Casey*
George and Mildred   *Johnnie Mortimer and Brian Cooke*
Emmerdale Farm   *Douglas Watkinson*

City Life
Lies I, II   *Willy Russell*
Uncle Sangi   *Tom Hadaway*
Short Back and Sides I, II   *Alan Plater*

Communities
Shove Up a Bit   *Gavin Blakeney*
Hush-a-Bye   *Gavin Blakeney*
Blind Eye   *Gavin Blakeney*
Old Fogey   *Julia Jones*
Nuts and Bolts   *Julia Jones*

Situation Comedy
The Liver Birds   *Carla Lane*
Happy Ever After   *John Chapman and Eric Merriman*
Rising Damp   *Eric Chappell*
Last of the Summer Wine   *Roy Clarke*
Going Straight   *Dick Clement and Ian le Frenais*

Love and Marriage
Gulpin   *Sheila Fay and Ken Jones*
First Date   *David Williams*
The Fight   *David Williams*
Just Love   *Leonard Kingston*
I Cried at your Wedding   *Madeline Sotheby*
Mum, Where are You?   *Eric Paice*

Power
A Little Patch of Ground   *Geoffrey Case*
The Protectors   *Cherry Potter*
Power   *Ludus*
My Sister's Eighteenth   *John McGrath*
Pantomime   *Derek Walcott*

School
Grange Hill   *Phil Redmond*
The Little Dissident   *George Baker*
Maids the Mad Shooter   *Farrukh Dhondy*
Headmaster   *John Challen*
Name in the Papers   *David Williams*

Situation Comedy 2
Open All Hours   *Roy Clarke*
Only When I Laugh   *Eric Chappell*
Hancock's Half Hour   *Ray Galton and Alan Simpson*
A Fine Romance   *Bob Larbey*
Yes Minister   *Anthony Jay and Jonathan Lynn*

Scully   *Alan Bleasdale*
Scripts of the full seven-episode serial

Boys from the Blackstuff   *Alan Bleasdale*
Scripts of the full five-episode series